CREATING NEW MONEY

A monetary reform for the information age

Joseph Huber and James Robertson

CONTENTS

CONTENTS (contd)

ABOUT THE AUTHORS

Joseph Huber Born in 1948. Chair of economic and environmental sociology at Martin-Luther-University, Halle. Topics of research are industrial ecology as well as monetary policy. During the 70s and 80s he was an activist of the alternative movement and co-founder of Self-Help Network in Germany, a citizens' initiative pioneering in green banking and ethical investment. Before tenure in 1991, he earned his living as a writer and policy advisor. In recent years he has been active in the International Greening of Industry Network, the Environment Bank, and the Senate of Berlin Town Forum. He is co-founder of Citizens' Town AG Berlin.

Contact   Prof. Dr. Joseph Huber , Institut für Soziologie
               Martin-Luther-Universität, D – 06099 Halle
               Tel: +49 345 552.4242 Fax: +49 345 552.7149
               Email: huber@soziologie.uni-halle.de
               Internet: http://www.soziologie.uni-halle.de/huber/

James Robertson Born in 1928. Since 1973, independent writer, lecturer and consultant on alternative futures, economic and social change. Co-founder, New Economics Foundation, 1985. Recent publications include The New Economics of Sustainable Development (for the European Commission, 1999), and Transforming Economic Life (for the Schumacher Society in association with New Economics Foundation, 1998).

His early career had been in Whitehall; he accompanied Harold Macmillan on his prime-ministerial "Wind of Change" tour of Africa in 1960, and then worked in the Cabinet Office. He later set up and directed the Inter-Bank Research Organisation for the UK banks, and contributed to enquiries on government, civil service, parliament, and London's future as a financial centre.

Contact   James Robertson, The Old Bakehouse, Cholsey
               Oxon OX10 9NU, England
               Tel: +44 (0)1491 652346 Fax: +44 (0)1491 651804
               Email: robertson@tp2000.demon.co.uk

ACKNOWLEDGEMENTS

Our thanks are due to many people with whom we have discussed or corresponded about the matters covered in this report. For both of us they include Alan Armstrong, Richard Douthwaite, Brian Leslie and Ronnie Morrison.

James Robertson would like to thank the following for encouragement and stimulus: Peter Challen and his colleagues from the Christian Council for Monetary Justice, Aart de Lange and colleagues at SANE (Cape Town), Richard Douthwaite's colleagues at FEASTA (Dublin), James Gibb Stuart and other members of the "Bromsgrove Group", Martine Hamon, David Heathfield, Frances Hutchinson, William Krehm of COMER (Toronto), Bernard Lietaer, and Mike Rowbotham.

Joseph Huber would like to thank Rolf Gocht, Jürgen Pahlke, both early contributors to seigniorage reform, as well as H.C. Binswanger, E.U. von Weizsacker, Philippe van Parijs and his colleagues from the Basic Income European Network, and Christopher H. Budd, for supportive comments and criticism.

We are grateful also to others, in organisations like the Bank of England, the European Central Bank and the German Bundesbank, who have responded helpfully to enquiries and correspondence.

Our special thanks are due to Ed Mayo, and to his Trustees and colleagues at the New Economics Foundation, for their support and assistance to us in commissioning and publishing our report. James Robertson particularly wishes to thank them for the opportunity to work with Joseph Huber on it. He believes that Huber's approach to restoring the prerogative of seigniorage as a source of public revenue marks the start of a new phase in the long history of money, and that in the coming years many other people will be inspired by it.

FOREWORD

For all the prominence and sophistication of share dealing and financial services in the new economy, it is rare that we ask questions of our money system itself. The way that we issue and use money seems so ingrained that it's hard to question. It is, in the words of George Orwell "the air we breathe". Like air, it's everywhere, we are dependent on it, and perhaps most important, until it is really dirty, it cannot be seen. We see the money system as something natural. But it's not.

The rules of the money system have shifted. The majority of money that now changes hands does so electronically. As a result, far more than ever before, new money is not issued by the state but by banks. Ninety seven pounds in every one hundred circulating in the economy will now have been issued by banks (in the form of sight deposits, printed into customers' accounts as interest-bearing debts). Only three pounds are cash, issued by the state (in the form of banknotes and coins, issued at no interest). The cost to the state of issuing new money is only the cost of producing banknotes and coins. The cost to the banks of issuing new money is virtually zero. The state receives public revenues from issuing cash, but banks make private profits. The benefits of the money system are therefore being captured by the financial services industry rather than shared democratically.

The loss of this privilege is equivalent to an extraordinary twelve pence on income tax in the UK. In effect it has become a subsidy to the private banking sector – a nice little earner, but one that should always have been for public benefit rather than private gain. This is likely to grow as as we move further still towards a cash-free economy, perhaps to a point where coins and notes represent less than 1% of money in circulation. Unless we find creative alternatives, the benefit of issuing new money will have transferred entirely from public benefit into private corporate gain.

This argument has been made by monetary reformers, who have become increasingly vocal. The contemporary Jubilee 2000 campaign, for example, focuses on the unpayable debts of the poorest countries. It has begun to argue that debt is as systemic a by-product as pollution or global warming of a global political economy locked into the search for rates of return on capital of fifteen per cent annually or more.

This report represents a fundamental breakthrough on this agenda. While the principles of monetary reform have been asserted often enough before, the steps from where we are to where we need to be, in terms of a democratic and efficient money system, have been obscure or unconvincing.

For the first time, this report offers a practical and clear step-by-step agenda on the essential first step of restoring the right of issuing new money in a modern economy to be of benefit for the common good. In the terms of the new thinking that is emerging about the creation of sustainable and inclusive economies, this is an achievement that ranks high. It fits directly into a new theoretical model, combining socio- and ecological economics, in which market actors are located within common property resources rather than allowed to free-ride on the back of them. In short, the market meets the commons; and new economics, whether through eco-taxes or monetary reform, concerns the achievement of a fairer and more sustainable balance of cost, risk and return between the two.

This report addresses the issues and the complexities of how new money can be created. I encourage you to engage with it in full, because the analysis and prescriptions are landmark achievements and I am proud to be associated with it.

There is no better time for an idea such as monetary reform to flourish. The democratic state is being eroded in the face of global markets. In many parts of the world, concerns about market failure now have to be put alongside concerns about state failure. Issuing new money in the form of public expenditure enables the public purse to go further – whether for public transport, environment or regeneration. Restoring democratic control over how new money is issued is an important step towards a global economy in which unpayable debts are reduced and resources can be freed up for sustainable development.

Many of the ideas developed by the New Economics Foundation and sister organisations working on sustainability around the world seemed obscure or unlikely when we first set them out. We look forward to monetary reform moving to the centre stage of public and policy debate in the way that eco-taxes, stakeholding and debt cancellation have done. We invite your participation, whether as a critic or as a supporter, in helping to shape this debate for the economy of our future.

Ed Mayo, Executive Director New Economics Foundation

Chapter 1

A MONETARY REFORM FOR THE INFORMATION AGE

*"A change was coming upon the world – a change from era to era.
The paths trodden by the footsteps of ages were broken up; old things
were passing away."*

J.A. Froude, *History of England.*

Today's monetary and banking system is, in essence, still based on the
500 year old fractional reserve system suited to metal money. It still has
to catch up with the new payment practices and the accelerating
circulation of non-cash money based on modern information and
telecommunication technology.

It is now opaque, inherently unsafe and unstable, almost impossible to
control, and too expensive. It is increasingly perceived as part of an
unaccountable system of money and finance that needs reform at every
level – local, national and international. New initiatives and proposals are
in the air. The New Economics Foundation has been prominent in
developing and promoting LETS (local exchange trading systems), time
money and other alternative or parallel currencies, microcredit,
community banking, credit unions, and other new approaches to local
community finance (Mayo *et al* 1998).

The reform we discuss in this report is different from those. It is not
directly linked to them, but is a wider issue. It is a reform of the
mainstream monetary and banking system. It reflects the values of a
democratic civil society and the need for economic and financial stability.
It is in tune with the Information Age.

It is basically simple. It is in two parts.

1. Central banks should create the amount of new non-cash money (as
    well as cash) they decide is needed to increase the money supply, by
    crediting it to their governments as public revenue. Governments
    should then put it into circulation by spending it.

2. It should become infeasible and be made illegal for anyone else to create new money denominated in an official currency. Commercial banks will thus be excluded from creating new credit as they do now, and be limited to credit-broking as financial intermediaries.

We refer to this as "seigniorage reform". While adapting to the new conditions of the Information Age, it will also restore the prerogative of the state to issue legal tender, and to capture as public revenue the seigniorage income that arises from issuing it. Originally, seigniorage arose from the minting and issuing of coins by monarchs and local rulers. Extending it to the creation of all official money will correct the anomaly that has grown up over the years, resulting today in 95% of new money being issued, not by governments as cash (coins and banknotes), but by commercial banks printing credit entries into the bank accounts of their customers in the form of interest-bearing loans. This costs the public large sums of money in seigniorage revenue foregone, in the UK, for example, of the order of £47bn a year (Appendix, Table 4G). It gives the commercial banks a hidden subsidy in the shape of special, supernormal profits of the order of £21bn a year in the UK (Appendix, Table 4B). We estimate that, in total, the resulting cost burden for the UK economy is about £66bn a year (Appendix, Table 4E).

Chapter 2 outlines the arrangements that seigniorage reform will introduce for creating new non-cash money and putting it into circulation. It will be a two-stage process. First, central banks will issue the new money as public revenue by entering it into the current accounts they hold for their governments.[1] Second, governments will spend it into circulation.

It will be for central banks to decide at regular intervals how much new money to issue. They will make their decisions in accordance with monetary policy objectives that have previously been laid down and published, and they will be accountable for their performance. But they will have a high degree of independence from government, giving governments no power to intervene in decisions about how much new money to create. Scaremongers will raise the spectre of inflation. But we show that, among other benefits, seigniorage reform can be expected to provide more effective safeguards against the risk of inflation than exist today, when commercial banks print almost all the new money.

There are many ways in which governments will be able to spend the new money into circulation. We discuss some of these, e.g. paying off the National Debt, or reducing taxation. But we conclude that, in principle, what governments do with this revenue should – as with other public revenue – be a matter which the government of the day should decide in accordance with its priorities. Whatever decisions governments take in this respect, seigniorage reform will have a very beneficial effect on public finance.

Chapter 3 explains how commercial banks will be prevented from printing new money. Four comparatively straightforward changes will be needed, as follows.

- Sight deposits denominated in the official currency will be recognised as legal tender, along with cash.

- The total amount of non-cash money existing in all current accounts (including those of bank customers, banks, and government), together with the total amount of cash in everyone's possession, will be recognised as constituting the total stock of official money or legal tender immediately available for spending.

- Customers' current accounts will be taken off the banks' balance sheets, and the banks' will manage them separately from their own money (which is not what they do today). As a result, a clear distinction will be introduced between means-of-payment money ("plain money")[2] in current accounts, and store-of-value money ("capital") in savings accounts. In practice this will mean that, except when a central bank is creating new money as public revenue, payments into current accounts will always have to be matched by payments out of other current accounts, or paid in as cash.

- Finally, if any person or organisation other than a central bank fails to observe that distinction and prints new non-cash legal tender into a current account, they will be guilty of counterfeiting or forgery – just as they would be if they manufactured unauthorised banknotes or coins.

Until now, bankers, monetary officials of government, mainstream monetary academics, and even most monetary reformers, have accepted what everyone knows to have become fiction. The truth now is that bank sight deposits and banknotes – which in the UK still say "I promise to pay…" – signify more than merely an entitlement to money. They actually are money.

So, for example, the reserve system for controlling the creation of new non-cash money by banks has to be seen as a throwback to a time when money was a physical substance, gold or silver, and not primarily – as now – information held in bank accounts and transmitted directly from one bank account to another. As goldsmiths and bankers increasingly lent greater amounts of credit than the money they possessed themselves and than had been deposited with them for safekeeping, it was recognised as prudent – and then became obligatory – to limit the total amount of credit they gave to a specified multiple of the gold and silver they held in reserve. That gold and silver, and subsequently the other immediately liquid assets which took their place, became known as a "fractional reserve" – because it was a specified fraction of the total value of the credit a bank could give. The system of banking management and control based on it became known as "fractional reserve banking".

As Chapter 3 describes, proposals for monetary reform have often advocated 100% banking (in place of fractional reserve banking) as a way to prevent banks creating new money. Failure to get those proposals adopted has been at least partly due to the difficulty of implementing them, reflecting as they did an out-of-date understanding of the changed nature of money and the process of creating it. The plain money proposal will achieve the same aim as 100% banking would have done, but in a simpler way – easier to understand and implement, and more fully reflecting the nature of money in the Information Age.

Finally in Chapter 3 – and later in greater depth in the Appendix – we discuss the clarification of monetary statistics, monetary definitions and monetary terminology which seigniorage reform will prompt, and which is desirable for its own sake. With the blurring of the distinction between means-of-payment money and store-of-value money – i.e. between the functions of sight deposits and savings deposits – that has taken place in recent decades, the definitions on which monetary understanding and policy-making are based have become correspondingly muddled. For example, it is not at all clear what is now meant by the "money supply". The different definitions of money – M0, M1, etc, up to M4 – are abracadabra to most people. One sometimes feels that, if a banking priesthood had deliberately designed monetary statistics and terminology to conceal from citizens and politicians of democratic countries how the money system now works and how it could be made to work for the common good, they would have been hard put to improve on what exists today!

Having shown in Chapter 2 that the impact of seigniorage reform on public finance – taxation, public borrowing and public spending – will be highly beneficial, in **Chapter** 4 we discuss some of the wider advantages claimed for it.

Among possible advantages are:

▶ greater equity and social justice

▶ reducing inflationary tendencies in the economy

▶ creating greater economic stability by reducing the peaks and troughs of business cycles

▶ improving the safety and stability of domestic banking institutions

▶ removing distortions caused by channelling 95% of new money into the investment and spending priorities of banks and their customers

▶ reducing monetary pressures and constraints arising from the creation of new money by commercial banks as interest-bearing debt, that encourage environmentally unsustainable development, and

▶ a monetary and banking system that is transparent and open to public and political understanding of how it works.

Chapter 5 deals with various suggested objections to the proposal for seigniorage reform. Some – e.g. that it will mean nationalising the banks and putting a tax on money – can be briskly dismissed as obvious misconceptions, and – as explained in Chapters 2 and 4 – seigniorage reform is likely to reduce, not increase, tendencies to inflation.

Examination of the possible impact of seigniorage reform on banking services and banking profitability shows that any negative effects on the services banks can offer, or on their ability to compete in domestic markets, will be outweighed by the benefits of the reform. Study of the suggestion that it will be possible to evade or bypass the prohibition on the creation of new official money by anyone except the central bank shows that risks of evasion by conventional banks will be limited and can be minimised; and suggests that the risks of monetary controls being bypassed by a growing use of parallel currencies, or by the development of electronic currencies and internet banking, will actually be smaller after seigniorage reform than they would have been without it.

Finally, there is the suggested objection that the citizens, businesses, banks and economy of a country or currency area that initiates seigniorage reform might be at a disadvantage in international financial affairs. Again, examination shows that the advantages of reform are likely to outweigh any disadvantages in that respect. Moreover, it is possible that seigniorage reform will help to strengthen international monetary and financial stability, and provide a model which could be relevant to the further development of the international monetary system for a globalised economy.

Chapter 6 assesses the prospects for seigniorage reform, and discusses what should be done to promote it. As always, the minority who will lose by it will strongly resist it, whereas the majority who will benefit from it will tend to be more lukewarm in their support. Who will be its opponents, and who its beneficiaries and supporters? What trigger issues and events may help to spread wider understanding of it and support for it? Which countries could take the lead in pioneering it? And why may it be possible to achieve it now, when similar attempts have been successfully resisted for the past two centuries? Our answers to these questions are realistic but optimistic.

Support will be needed from people in the following groups:

- politicians and public officials, not necessarily connected with banking and financial affairs;
- the banking industry itself, the central banks, and other national and international monetary and banking institutions;

- the mainstream community of economic and financial policy-makers, policy-analysts, policy-debaters and policy-commentators;

- the community of respected monetary academics, monetary historians and other specialist monetary and banking experts;

- the wider community of individuals, NGOs and pressure groups, who are committed to the support of proposals for greater economic efficiency which involve a fairer sharing of resources, but who may as yet be unfamiliar with the relevance of monetary reform; and

- the community of already committed supporters of monetary reform.

We hope this report will attract the attention of monetary and banking experts and policy makers. But it is often difficult for people pursuing a professional career in a particular walk of life to take a positive interest in proposals for its reform until there is widespread recognition that they should. We suggest, therefore, that bodies like the New Economics Foundation should give high priority to spreading awareness of the case for seigniorage reform among politicians and public officials, and potentially interested individuals, NGOs and pressure groups. They, together with existing supporters of monetary reform, can then help to create a climate of informed opinion that will make it easier – indeed more compelling – for the experts to give seigniorage reform the serious attention it demands.

Endnotes

1   Current accounts contain sight deposits (or demand deposits or overnight deposits) in which non-cash money is immediately available as a means of payment. In that respect they differ from savings (or time deposit) accounts, sometimes known simply as deposit accounts. The current accounts held by central banks for commercial banks are known as operational accounts. For further details see Appendix, Section A.1.

2   We use the term "plain money" to refer to official money (legal tender), both cash and non-cash in current accounts. After seigniorage reform "the stock of plain money" will more plainly define the money supply than any term now in use. See Huber 1999.

Chapter 2

RESTORING SEIGNIORAGE:

IMPLICATIONS FOR PUBLIC FINANCE AND MONETARY POLICY

"The privilege of creating and issuing money is not only the supreme prerogative of government, but it is the government's greatest creative opportunity."

Abraham Lincoln, 1865.

This chapter outlines the proposed method of issuing new money and putting it into circulation, and the implications for public finance. It also explains how the existing approach to monetary control can be adapted to ensure that the new method of issuing money will involve no more risk of inflation than continuing to allow the commercial banks to issue it.

In summary, central banks will take over from the commercial banks the function of issuing new non-cash money for public circulation. In doing so they will act in accordance with published policy objectives and be accountable for their performance, but they will have a high degree of independence. Governments must have no power to intervene in the decisions of central banks on how much new money to create.

The proposed method of creating new money will be simpler, more straightforward and easier to understand than the present one. It will be markedly beneficial from the viewpoint of public spending, borrowing and taxation. Subject to one proviso, it will almost certainly provide a more effective and practical instrument of monetary control. The proviso is that the creation of new money by commercial banks shall stop. Chapter 3 will deal with that aspect.

2.1 Method of Issuing New Money

New non-cash money will be issued and put into circulation in the following way.

The first step will be for a central bank simply to write it into a current account which it manages for its government (or, in the case of the European Central Bank, the current accounts which it manages for its governments). Instead of the commercial banks printing the new money into their customers' accounts, the central banks will be entering it into the accounts of their governments. A central bank will probably make these payments to its government at regular two- or four-week intervals, not necessarily at constant amounts. Most importantly, it will make them as debt-free payments – outright grants – not as interest-bearing loans.

For example, in the UK, USA, Japan and other countries, the national central banks will make these payments into accounts which they manage for the Treasury or Finance Ministry of their respective national governments. In the Eurozone the European Central Bank (ECB) will make the payments into accounts which it manages for the national governments of member states. The ECB could distribute the total between member states in proportion to their national population, or in proportion to their national Gross Domestic Product (GDP), or according to a mixture of the two – this third possibility reflecting the formula that governs the proportions in which the share capital of the ECB is held by each national central bank.[1] The basis for distribution will be decided by member states and the ECB as part of their decision to create new money debt-free as public revenue.

The second step will be for governments to spend the new money into circulation, just as they spend other public revenue – on public expenditure programmes such as education, defence, servicing the national debt, etc, etc.

Issuing new non-cash money will thus have become a source of public revenue, as issuing cash already is. This will enable governments to increase public spending, or to reduce taxation or government borrowing, or both in combination. As can be seen (Appendix, Table 4, lines J and L), the amounts will be significant – of the order of £48bn in the UK, $114bn in the USA, more than €160bn in the Euro area, and more than ¥17 trillion in Japan. These figures amount to 5–15% of annual tax revenues in the major OECD countries.

Decisions about how to use this revenue will be for governments to take, according to their political principles. Left-of-centre governments will tend to prefer increases in public spending, whereas right-of-centre governments will tend to prefer tax reductions. Owing to the great increase in public spending, taxation and borrowing over the past century and a half, the creative opportunities offered by seigniorage reform today may not seem quite so dramatic as they did to Abraham Lincoln. But governments of all persuasions will welcome it.

2.2 Government Spending

How, then, should governments spend the new money into circulation? Some supporters of monetary reform have suggested that governments should channel it through one particular public spending programme rather than others. One suggestion is that the money should be used to reduce and eventually pay off the National Debt altogether, thus reducing and eventually eliminating the need for taxes or further borrowing to pay interest on it (e.g. Gibb Stuart 1995). C.H. Douglas and others have suggested that the new money should be put into circulation as a national dividend or citizen's income (see e.g. Armstrong 1996). This would provide a basic weekly or monthly income to every citizen as a right. That would reflect the entitlement of every citizen to share in the monetary value of common resources – a point we shall discuss further in 4.1.

A third suggestion is that government should put the new money into circulation in the form of interest-free loans, e.g. to local government for development. A State and Local Government Economic Empowerment Act (HR1452) was recently introduced in the US Congress.[2] It would enable the federal government to create money to give interest-free loans to state and local governments to finance infrastructure building and repair. This would mean big savings for taxpayers – half to a third of the cost of raising interest-bearing municipal bonds. Growing numbers of Congressmen are co-sponsoring the bill, and it has been attracting support from bankers, economists, accountants, academics and others. Such loans, although interest-free, would not reflect the principle that new money should be put into circulation debt-free. Nonetheless, in terms of political practice, this approach might be a useful halfway house

– helping to establish the principle that new non-cash money should be created and put into circulation for public purposes.

Although we agree on the desirability of reducing the National Debt, and on the arguments – economic, social and environmental – for a citizen's income, we see no reason to insist that the new seigniorage revenue should necessarily be spent into circulation on some particular purposes as opposed to others. How the government should spend it does not affect, and should not be confused with, the principle that new money should be created as debt-free public revenue and not as debt-constituting banking industry assets. When that principle has been accepted and the arrangements for creating new money as public revenue are settled, the question of how the revenue is to be spent will be a matter of government budgetary policy and political decision in the ordinary way.

2.3 Government Borrowing

One result of the government's failure to collect seigniorage revenue from issuing non-cash money is that it has to borrow more than it otherwise would. This has re-inforced the tendency of rulers everywhere in every age to spend more, whether for purposes of princely luxury, warfare or public welfare, than they could raise in tax revenues. Over the 20th century, government debt in all countries has risen, up to 50–60% of GDP in the UK, the USA, France or Germany, 85% in Japan, and 115–130% in Greece, Italy, or Belgium. As a result, a growing proportion of the annual tax revenue is now being used to pay interest on and redeem the public debt. At present this proportion accounts for about 10–15% of national government expenditure in most of the industrialised countries.

The suggestion is sometimes made that, when government has recovered the power to create new money and put it into circulation as public spending, it will no longer have to borrow any money at all; the central bank will be able to print and give it all it needs. We do not agree with this for the following reasons.

First, it will still be necessary, as now, to safeguard against contributing to inflation by creating too much money. The normal and regular way to finance government budgets will unavoidably continue to be by levying taxes and charges – and revenue from such sources as sales of licences, for example to provide the next generation of mobile phone services which recently raised £22.5bn for the UK government.

Second, there is no reason to prohibit government from raising long-term loans to finance capital investment in infrastructure. Sometimes that may be the fairest way to share the cost between present and future taxpayers, if the debt can be serviced and repaid in future years out of charges on users of the infrastructure or out of higher tax revenues arising from the increased prosperity the investment will help to create.

Third, although to some extent the creation of new money debt-free may be expected to reduce the amplitude of economic or business cycles and smooth out their peaks and troughs (see 4.5), those cycles will no doubt continue to occur. This means there will continue to be periods of comparatively lower prosperity and comparatively higher unemployment in which tax revenues will fall and recurrent public expenditure (e.g. on social benefits) will rise. There will also continue to be seasonal imbalances between inward flows of public revenue and outward flows of public expenditure. To meet the resulting revenue gaps, governments will continue to need to borrow short- and medium-term. The resulting loans should be repaid in subsequent periods of higher tax revenue and lower public expenditure. The important point is that, over an economic cycle as a whole, all government debt raised to finance recurrent public expenditure should be repaid and no increase in the National Debt should result. This reflects what has recently become known in the UK as 'the golden rule': "Over the economic cycle, the government will borrow only to invest and not to fund current spending". [3]

However, although seigniorage reform will not bring government borrowing to an end, it will have beneficial consequences for it. Specifically, it will mean that governments will no longer borrow and pay interest on money from the banks, which they have allowed the banks to print for the purpose of lending it to them.

2.4 Taxation

Governments will, as we have said, have the option to use the new seigniorage revenue to reduce taxation. This is important at a time of pressure to reduce existing taxes.

In an increasingly competitive global economy, the growing mobility of capital and highly qualified people is pressing national governments to reduce taxes on incomes, profits and capital. In an ageing society, opposition is likely to grow to taxing fewer people of working age on the fruits of their efforts, in order to support a growing number of "economically inactive" people. Internet trading ("e-commerce") will make it more difficult for national governments to collect customs duties, value added tax and other taxes and levies on sales, especially on products and services that can be downloaded from the internet. It will also make it easier for businesses and people to shift their earnings and profits to low-tax regimes.

These pressures are combining with other economic, social and environmental arguments to support a tax shift – shifting the burden of taxes off enterprise and employment and on to the use of resources, including land, energy and the capacity of the environment to absorb pollution. There is also the demand of international bodies like the OECD and the EU for action to reduce the attractions of tax havens. A more effective way of reducing them, rather than trying to enforce internationally harmonised regulations for the collection of existing taxes, might be by a tax shift which will reduce existing levels of tax on incomes, profits and capital.

Apart from the option to use some of the new seigniorage revenue to replace existing taxes, one further point should be noted. Supporters of land value taxation, i.e. taxing the site value of land, claim similar advantages for it as are claimed for monetary reform (on which see Chapter 4): it will help to smooth out the peaks and troughs of economic cycles, make it possible to reduce distortionary taxes that now damage the economy, distribute more fairly the value of resources that should be shared in common, and open up opportunities for enterprise and work to people now excluded from them.

Unfortunately, instead of co-operating with one another to promote these complementary reforms, there has been a tendency among some supporters of land value taxation and monetary reform to dispute which of the two is the more important. Further study of possible links and interactions between the two might encourage a coalition of support for both. This could usefully be initiated by a body such as the New Economics Foundation.

2.5 Monetary Control and Inflation

The amount of new money created as a source of public revenue will have to be effectively controlled. Increases in the quantity of money in circulation will have to accord strictly and clearly with the amounts judged necessary to meet the objectives of monetary policy. At present the main objective of monetary policy is to keep inflation under control. It will therefore be essential to guard, and be seen to guard, against the risk of contributing to inflation by creating too much money.

This needs to be stressed – for two reasons. First, although too much money is not the only cause of inflation, as proponents of a pure quantity theory of money might sometimes appear to suggest, it can certainly be a contributory cause. Second, it is almost always suggested by opponents of monetary reform that printing new money as a source of public revenue risks being more inflationary than having the banks print it in the form of commercially profitable loans.

The solution is, in fact, straightforward. In order to insulate politicians from pressures to create too much new money, the amount to be created should be decided at regular intervals by a monetary authority with a high degree of independence. In the UK the natural candidate for the task will be the Bank of England's Monetary Policy Committee. In the Euro area it will be the European Central Bank; in the USA the Federal Reserve System; and in Japan the Bank of Japan. These bodies are now responsible for regulating the creation of new money by the commercial banks.

Section 2.6 will discuss the nature of the relationship between the functions and responsibilities of central monetary authorities and those of their governments. But first, this section establishes that it should be no more difficult for central monetary authorities to control the amounts of new money created by themselves as public revenue, than it is at present for them to control the amounts created by the banks as loans to their customers. In fact it should be easier.

Today the central banks, as central monetary authorities, manipulate short-term interest rates with the aim of controlling the amounts of new money put into circulation by the banks as loans to their customers. By raising interest rates a central bank aims to raise the cost of borrowing throughout the economy, thereby to reduce the demand for bank loans, and thereby to reduce the quantity of new money put into circulation by the banks. By lowering interest rates a central bank aims to reduce the cost of borrowing, thereby to increase the demand for bank loans, and thereby to increase the quantity of new money the banks create.

When, as hitherto, it is accepted unquestioningly that the way new money is created is by banks in the form of interest-bearing loans, then naturally enough – especially in the prevailing climate of deregulation and freer commercial markets of the 1980s and 1990s – it became the conventional wisdom that the best way to exercise monetary control is indirectly, i.e. via interest rates. The shift during that period in the UK, for example, away from direct controls on bank lending to indirect control of interest rates, is clearly summarised by the Bank of England (1998b).

However, once it is accepted that a better way to put new money into circulation is as interest-free contributions to public revenue rather than as bank loans, it will become possible for central banks to decide directly how much new money to create. They will no longer have to try to exercise control indirectly. Demand for money and the price of money will then respond, as in any free market, to the available supply, rather than vice versa as at present. The market for money will operate more freely and openly than today, the method of controlling the supply will be more open to public understanding, and the effects of monetary policy on businesses, employment and people's livelihoods will be less accidental.

In fact, Bank of England advisers accept that "there is no single, ideal structure of monetary policy targets or money market operations... One of the most fundamental issues is to decide which target to adopt: the quantity of money or its price, the rate of interest." (Bank of England 1996: 40)

Moreover, in explaining the "Transmission Mechanism of Monetary Policy", the Bank accepts that the money supply plays an important role in the transmission mechanism, although

> *"it is not, under the United Kingdom's monetary arrangements, a policy instrument. It could be a target of policy, but it need not be so. In the United Kingdom it is not, as we have an inflation target, and so monetary aggregates are indicators only. However, for each path of the official rate given by the decisions of the MPC, there is an implied path for the monetary aggregates. And in some circumstances, monetary aggregates might be a better indicator than interest rates of the stance of monetary policy. In the long run, there is a positive relationship between each monetary aggregate and the general level of prices. Sustained increases in prices cannot occur without accompanying increases in the monetary aggregates. It is in this sense that money is the nominal anchor of the system"*
>
> (Bank of England 1999: 10–11).

Thus it seems fairly clear that – insofar as monetary factors affect the rate of inflation – a central bank will find it easier, not more difficult, to control inflation if it has the responsibility and power to decide how much new money to create at regular intervals, rather than having to rely on variations in interest rates as its instrument of control. Moreover, as the present Governor of the Bank of England has stressed, monetary control in its present form "is a kind of art, not a science; it is an art which can be more or less carefully crafted but an art it is, nevertheless".[4] There appears no reason why central monetary authorities should be unable to develop the carefully crafted art needed to decide what regular increases should be made to the quantity of money in circulation.

This would still apply if the objectives of monetary policy were to change. At present the primary objective is to keep inflation under control. For example, in the UK the Chancellor of the Exchequer requires the

Monetary Policy Committe of the Bank of England to aim for a target annual inflation rate within a range either side of 2.5%. The Statute of the European System of Central Banks lays down that the "primary objective of the ESCB shall be to maintain price stability". The US Federal Reserve System is required to pursue "long-run objectives of price stability and sustainable economic growth".

This report is not about what the objectives of monetary policy should be. But some countries – including UK, US, Euro area, Japan – might decide sometime in the future that the objectives of their monetary policies should change, for example to try to control both inflation and the exchange rate to keep both within a specified range. In that event, will controlling the quantity of new money created interest-free as public revenue be as effective as regulating the price of money would have been? The foregoing discussion suggests that it will be at least as effective an instrument of control, and probably a more effective one, however monetary policy objectives may change from time to time.

2.6 Central Bank/Government Relations

In democratic societies the objectives of monetary policy, as of other public policies, must be decided and implemented in a democratically accountable way. But it should be emphasised again that political ministers and their officials should play no part in deciding how much new money should be created to meet those objectives. That should be decided at regular intervals by the central bank operating independently as the national (or Euro area) monetary authority.

Differing views exist about the degree of independence that the central bank should have from the government, what the relationship between government and central bank should be, and what institutional forms it should take. A brief discussion may be of interest here. But the crucial point is that, whatever answer different people may give to these questions, it will be an essential, integral part of seigniorage reform to ensure that the central monetary authorities' decisions on how much new money to create are independent of government interference.

In the UK the present relationship between the Chancellor of the Exchequer on the one hand and the Bank of England and its Monetary Policy Committee on the other, which was introduced by the present government three years ago, provides one model. Elected ministers and their officials are accountable to parliament for the overall objectives of monetary policy, and the central bank is independently accountable to parliament for the exercise of monetary control to achieve those objectives. At present the UK government has set a target for the Bank of England to keep the rate of inflation at 2.5%. If inflation should go more than 1% higher or lower than that, the Bank is required to publish the reasons why that has happened and how it proposes to correct it. In deciding what to do from time to time (e.g what interest-rate change to make, if any) in order to meet the target, the Bank acts with complete independence from elected ministers and their officials, and is itself directly accountable to Parliament for the way it carries out its task. Public discussion tends to interpret the Bank's degree of independence, and the fact that its committee is called the Monetary Policy Committee, as meaning that the government has handed over monetary policy to the Bank while keeping fiscal policy to itself. In a narrow sense that is true. But by retaining responsibility for deciding on the objective of monetary policy, the government has clearly retained an important monetary policy role.

Other models are perfectly possible, and some might argue preferable. The objectives of the central monetary authority might be laid down by law, they might be decided by the central monetary authority itself under some other form of democratic accountability, and no doubt other institutional arrangements will have their advocates. But whatever the model, a broad analogy can be drawn between the independence that courts of law and the central monetary authority should have. Although elected governments should be responsible for proposing laws for the approval of parliaments and be accountable to parliaments for changing the laws when they decide changes are necessary, the courts should be independently responsible for administering the laws without interference. Similarly, central monetary authorities (at present, central banks) should be independently responsible for deciding how much new money should be created with no interference from government, in a context of broad policy objectives that have been democratically approved.

Endnotes

1   Article 29.1 of the Statute of the European System of Central Banks and of the European Central Bank.

2   Details from Sovereignty, 1154 West Logan Street, Freeport, IL 61032, USA; chairman Ken Bohnsack Email: sovgntyken@aol.com.

3   "Analysing Fiscal Policy", HM Treasury, November 1999.

4   Answer to Question 54, Minutes of Evidence of the House of Commons Select Committee on the Treasury, meeting of Tuesday 23 February 1999.

Chapter 3

RESTORING SEIGNIORAGE:
IMPLICATIONS FOR BANKING

> *"The process by which banks create money is so simple that the mind is repelled. Where something so important is involved, a deeper mystery seems only decent."*

Galbraith, 1975.

Ending the creation of money by the banks will also be surprisingly simple. The monetary and financial institutions will stay the same. Almost all the everyday routines of the banking and financial markets will continue as if nothing had happened. No one's monetary possessions, including the banks', will be touched. Nothing will be expropriated.

Naturally, the reform will not be uncontroversial. But once the political will is there, the required legal and technical measures will be straightforward. Two things will need to be done. First, the prerogative of creating official money, i.e. the exclusive public right to create legal tender, will have to be extended to include sight deposits in current accounts as well as cash. Second, the banking sector will have to stop creating them.

3.1 Declaring Sight Deposits as Legal Tender

Enacting the public prerogative of creating official money will require a simple but fundamental change in the law. It is most clearly illustrated by the change needed in the Statute of the European System of Central Banks and the European Central Bank.

Article 16 of the European Statute is titled "Banknotes". It reads as follows:

> *"... The Governing Council shall have the exclusive right to authorise the issue of banknotes within the Community. The ECB and the national central banks may issue such notes. The banknotes issued by*

> *the ECB and the national central banks shall be the only such notes*
> *to have the status of legal tender within the Community."*

The changed version could be titled "Legal Tender". It will be on the
following lines:

> *"...The Governing Council shall have the exclusive right to authorise*
> *the issue of legal tender within the Community. Legal tender includes*
> *coin, banknotes, and sight deposits. The ECB and the national*
> *central banks may issue such means of payment. Coin, banknotes,*
> *and sight deposits issued by the ECB and the national central banks*
> *shall be the only means of payment to have the status of legal tender*
> *within the Community."*

The same change will need to be legislated in other countries. In principle
it will be identical, although the existing legislation may be somewhat
more complex. In the USA it will be necessary to amend further the 1913
Federal Reserve Act, Sec.16, as subsequently amended, and perhaps also
the US Constitution, Article 1, Sec. 8, Cl 5. In the UK further legislation
will be needed to bring up to date the series of Acts that started with the
1844 Bank Charter Act and has included the Acts nationalising the Bank
of England in 1946 and restructuring its functions in 1998.

Such a reformulation of the existing law will establish the prerogative of
creating official money in a contemporary form. It will put beyond doubt
that the institution in charge is the central bank, and that central banks
are no longer the private businesses they once were. They will be formally
recognised for what they now actually are: a public authority central to
the monetary system, responsible for creating and regulating the stock of
all official money within their territory. Traditionally this state prerogative
has applied to coins. It now generally applies to banknotes too.[1] It will be
extended to non-cash money. As the status of legal tender was extended
from coins to banknotes from the 18th century on, so it will now be
extended to sight deposits, reflecting the overwhelmingly important role
that non-cash money now plays in our lives. Thus seigniorage reform is
not about grafting unheard of ideas on to the monetary system. It is
about the logical extension to non-cash money – now the most important
kind of money – of well-established practice. It recognises what we all

know. Sight deposits denominated in the official currency now serve as money, as cash does; bits and bytes now complement coins and notes as media of monetary exchange.

3.2 How To Stop The Creation Of Sight Deposits By Commercial Banks

The second thing that needs to be achieved by seigniorage reform is to stop the creation of sight deposits by the commercial banking sector. Within the current reserve system, banks cannot be prevented from creating them – partly because of the technicalities of the existing conventions of bank accounting.

Different approaches have been put forward as a solution to the problem. One was the concept of stamp scrips invented by Silvio Gesell (1919) which attracted attention and support in Central Europe and the United States in the years around 1930. An equally influential programme of the 1920s and 1930s was the proposal of debt-free social credit put forward by C.H. Douglas (see Hutchinson/Burkitt 1997, Munson 1945, Mairet 1934). A more recent contribution is that of a general public prerogative of money creation put forward by Pahlke (1970) and Gocht (1975) independently of each other.

Among the predecessors of these reformers were two of the most eminent U.S. presidents. One was Thomas Jefferson (1743–1826) who was convinced that "the issuing power of money should be taken from the banks, and restored to the people to whom it belongs". The other was Abraham Lincoln (1809–1865) who urged that "the government should create, issue and circulate all the currency and credit needed to satisfy the spending power of the government and the buying power of consumers" (de Maré 1999).

Perhaps the most influential approach to monetary reform was the 100%-money proposal put forward by Irving Fisher (1935) also known as the plan for 100%-banking. It was called the Chicago plan after a group of Chicago economists, among them Henry Simons and later Milton Friedman (Simons 1948, Friedman 1948, 1959, 1969b, Hart 1935). The 100%-banking proposal continues to be seen as a possible answer to the problem, and has been the only reform approach respected inside the ivory towers of academia. The plan wanted the banks to be forced to hold a cash reserve of 100% matching every sight and savings deposit. These deposits, being non-cash, would be backed by cash holdings of the same amount. In this way deposits would become again the true and safe cash deposits they were thought to have formerly been.

The Fisher and Friedman proposals were important. But the weakness of the 100% plan was its failure to perceive that the nature and functions of money were now purely informational. Money had developed over the centuries from being special commodities, like gold, to being pure information. But the 100% reformers still saw money as cash – Fisher referred to cash as "actual physical money" (1935: 62). They wanted cash to play the traditional role that gold had played. They did not ask if it really made sense to back or "cover" one type of purely informational money that had been freely created ex nihilo, by another of the same kind. In this respect the Chicago plan was based on questionable concepts of money, deposits and capital. It also raised problems of how to manage the transition to 100%-banking and how to operate the new system. Not least, the plan was backward-looking, actually conserving the obsolete reserve system rather than overcoming it (details in Huber 1999).

The merits and historical interest of these past plans and proposals justify more academic study and research than they currently attract. But we shall not discuss in greater depth here how far the authors made lasting contributions to a better understanding of monetary affairs, how far they may have created fallacies of their own, and how far the appeal of their reform programmes in their time may have been overtaken historically by events and circumstances since then.

3.3 Bank Customers' Current Accounts

The solution is, in fact, simpler than those past proposals suggest. It follows directly from declaring sight deposits to be legal tender. It is to take bank customers' current accounts off bank balance sheets, and recognise formally what they now actually are: accounts containing non-cash money which belongs to customers, just as customers' wallets and purses contain cash money that belongs to them. In other words, customers' current accounts will cease to be accounts belonging to the banks. They will be containers of money belonging exclusively to bank customers.

Consider what this change will mean. At present, the origin of sight deposits in current accounts is a double loan – first, sight deposits have come into existence as a loan of a bank to a customer; thereafter, as they continue to circulate as money, sight deposits are a loan of customers to the banks. They are a cash loan in the sense that customers for the most part do not "cash in" their money claims on the bank but prefer cashless payment by transfer of sight deposits. In both their aspects as a double loan, sight deposits are both an asset and a debt for banks and customers alike. That is why they are included on banks' balance sheets as liabilities to the customers, and why they increasingly attract interest – though at low rates.

Under seigniorage reform, the new status of sight deposits in current accounts will no longer be based upon their origin as double loans. Money will enter into circulation as debt-free seigniorage. So the debt or liability feature of current accounts will disappear, whereas the asset feature for customers will remain – with sight deposits as official means of payment belonging to the holders of the accounts. Thus, sight deposits will become what the amended law will require them to be: plain non-cash money – actual money and not, from the banks' point of view, a claim to be repaid money or a liability to eventually have to pay out cash.

So a simple legal declaration will convert traditional sight deposits from being part of the banks' balance sheets, to being current accounts containing non-cash money managed by banks as a service to their customers. It should come into force on the same set date as the change in the law on legal tender.

By detaching current accounts from the banks' balance sheet, the problem of how to prevent banks from creating non-cash money will be solved. Banks need not be forbidden to create sight deposits. They will no longer be able to. As a direct consequence of the conversion, bank loans to their customers will be paid by banks out of their own already existing stock of plain money held in their current accounts (operational accounts) with the central bank, into the current accounts of their borrowing customers. Those accounts will merely be managed by banks for their customers, as a basis for the payments services and cash facilities which the banks will provide and manage for them. The money in them will no more be part of the bank's own business, than banknotes in a person's wallet are, or than the bonds and shares a bank or a stock broker may be managing for a customer belong to the bank or broker. Once the transitional period is over (see 3.4 and 3.6 below), the banks' aggregate current accounts of customers as they exist today will entirely cease to be part of their balance sheets. They will become a separate statistic showing the amount of non-cash money belonging to customers in current accounts managed for them by the banks.

In this way, seigniorage reform as we envisage it will achieve very simply what the earlier proposal for 100% banking was designed to achieve in a much more cumbersome way.

3.4 Banks' Current Accounts and Balance Sheets

After seigniorage reform the sight deposits of businesses and private persons in current accounts at banks will have become legal tender, as the sight deposits of banks in operational accounts (i.e. current accounts) at the central bank already are. Just as banks will manage those non-cash money accounts and cash facilities on behalf of their current account customers, so the central bank will manage them for the banks.

A bank's own money will exist either as cash in the bank's till or as non-cash money in its operational account with the central bank. When banks wish to make loans to customers, they will finance the loans by taking the money from their own tills or accounts. The greater part of that money will have been borrowed for the purpose by the banks from bank customers and other banks. It will be transferred from customer-lenders' current accounts at their bank (or from bank-lenders' operational accounts at the central bank), into the loan-broking bank's account at the central bank, and thence into the current account of the borrowing customer. The stock of circulating money will thus remain unchanged – except for the additions created by the central bank and spent into circulation as public expenditure, as described in Chapter 2. That will be the context in which banks will continue to be money brokers – loan-facilitating intermediaries – but no longer creators of sight deposits.

As we have said, with effect from the set date the sight deposits in current accounts of bank customers will no longer be liabilities of the banks to their customers, and will no longer be a claim of the customers against the banks that manage their accounts. The sight deposits will have become plain non-cash money and, by becoming unequivocal owners of this money, the customers will have fully satisfied their claims.

However, although no longer liabilities of the banks to their customers, those sight deposits will still be liabilities of the banks. They will have been converted at the set date into liabilities to the central bank. This will reflect the origin of the sight deposits then existing – as non-cash money created by commercial banks when they were performing the money-creating function proper to the central bank. It will recognise that, under seigniorage reform, that money would have been issued by the central bank, and that – because it was not so issued – it needs to be phased out. Otherwise it would constitute a huge unjustified windfall profit for the banks. It will be phased out by the banks repaying it to the central bank over a transitional period, as their customers repay old bank-loans to them. The amount of old credit creations will be the same as the amount of sight deposits existing at the set date. When that amount has been paid off by the banks to the central bank, the commercial banks' liabilities arising from their creation of credit will have been dissolved. The transition period will be over. The age of debt-free money will have arrived.

3.5 Central Banks' Accounts and Balance Sheets

After the set date, then, the balance sheets of commercial banks will continue to show their loans to loan-taking customers as assets. In fact, the asset side of banks' balance sheets will not change very much. Change will be greater on the liabilities side, as banks will have to borrow all the money they lend to their customers and will no longer be able to create a considerable part of it.

As already explained, the liabilities of banks to their current account customers will be converted on the set date into liabilities to the central bank. Those liabilities will be matched by claims of the central bank on the banks, and those claims will be shown on the balance sheet of the central bank as assets. This will be a temporary arrangement, for the transitional period. As the claims are paid off by the banks to the central bank, the banks' liabilities in this respect and the central bank's matching assets will diminish and ultimately be extinguished. The old money created as debt will have been phased out. It will have been replaced by debt-free money created by the central bank and put into circulation as public expenditure.

The next question is this. As it issues the new debt-free money and credits it to the government's account, how will the central bank account for it?

With the move to debt-free money, central banks will need to keep separate their function of creating new money from their other functions of regulating or influencing or managing current flows of existing money in the financial markets. The Bank of England already distinguishes between the activities of its Issue Department and its Banking Department. But other important central banks still continue to keep these activities on the same balance sheet. After seigniorage reform this would mean mixing up debt-creating, interest-bearing activities with non-debt-creating and non-interest-bearing ones. Separating the issue account from the banking balance sheet will make the creation of money completely transparent. It will be clear that the issuing activities of central banks are creating new money, but their banking activities are not.

After seigniorage reform, the issue department of the central bank will regularly publish how much cash and non-cash money has been issued and to whom it has been issued. Normally it will have been credited as seigniorage to the Treasury (or Finance Ministry), but there may also be occasions when sums are issued as non-interest-bearing loans to the central bank's banking department. According to existing accounting conventions, seigniorage to the government and loans to the banking department would appear on the asset side of the issue department's balance sheet, matched on the liabilities side by the amounts of coin, notes, and sight deposits the issue department has paid out to finance the seigniorage and loans it has granted. So both sides of the issue balance would represent the existing stock of money, with the asset side indicating to whom the money was issued, and the liability side reflecting the amounts of issued coin, notes and sight deposits. However, it will need to be considered whether "asset/receivable" and "liability/debit" will still be appropriate terms for the meaning of the monetary items entered into the accounts of a central bank's issue department.[2] The issue department already is, and will be more completely so, the only institution authorised to spend official money without having taken it in before.

The banking department's monetary policy and foreign exchange activities will continue much as now, e.g. carrying out open market operations for short-term fine-tuning of the money supply, temporarily absorbing money from the banks or providing them with short-term loans when necessary in order to avoid excessively volatile interest rates in the interbank market (but only as an exception to the general rule that central banks will no longer provide money to the banks), and taking whatever steps may be thought necessary from time to time to pursue the objectives of monetary policy.

As a result, the balance sheet of the central bank's banking department will remain quite similar to other banking balance sheets of today. On the asset side there will be the amounts of:

- money borrowed from the issue department:
- available money temporarily taken in from the banks;
- available reserves of foreign exchange;
- receivables from limited overdraft loans made to banks; and
- receivables from foreign reserves lent on the open market.

On the liability side there will be the debts to be paid back to banks or the issue department – the latter being money borrowed for granting limited loans or buying foreign exchange.

Gold will almost certainly continue to take an increasingly unimportant place among the assets of a central bank. The metal age of money is over now. Central banks all round the world are already selling their stocks of gold, as discreetly as possible, and as slowly as necessary to avoid a gold-price collapse.

3.6 Only A Little "Big Bang"

To sum up, the introduction of seigniorage reform will start on a set date. From that date all new money will be issued by the central bank, and commercial banks will have to take up any new money they need by borrowing it at interest through the various channels available to them.

During a transitional period starting on that date, money that was created by the commercial banks will be phased out. The value to be phased out will be the total value of the sight deposits in current accounts held with all the banks on the set date. It will be phased out by each bank progressively redeeming what will now be its current account liabilities to the Issue Department at the central bank, as it receives repayment of existing loans it has made to its customers. So the conversion of traditional sight deposits into non-cash money will place no additional burdens on the banks. Their sight deposit liabilities will simply diminish until they reach zero.

The transition, then, will consist of phasing out old loans by paying them back via the banks to the central bank, to an amount identical with that of the sight deposits existing at the set date. There will be no institutional restructuring, simply a continuing phase-out of old loans to the point where the traditional credit base for special banking profits (see 4.1) has disappeared.

There is no reason why this conversion of traditional sight deposits into non-cash legal tender should disrupt banking business. The banks will have a conversion period of probably about five years, depending on how long it takes for the old bankloans to be paid back. If they wanted to, individual banks could be allowed to redeem their liabilities according to timetables individually negotiated with the central bank.

One of the questions that comes up in discussion is whether seigniorage reform will be a "big bang" or a process over time. The answer is that there will be what might be called a "big bang" at the set date, when the legal tender law will be amended and the conversion of current bank accounts will take place. This will then be followed by a transitional process of a technical nature in which old loans are phased out. "Big bang", though, is a dramatic term for a rather undramatic event, which will leave institutional and market structures untouched, and which will remain completely unnoticed by the money-using public unless they are told about it. It will only be a little "big bang", noticeable at the time mainly to the banks and the central bank whose accounts and procedures it will modify – but with quietly benign effects for almost everyone in the years that follow.

Endnotes

1 In many countries, consolidating the exclusive right of the central bank to issue banknotes has been a long historical process of piecemeal legislative and institutional change – in some cases not yet fully achieved, and also excluding coins. In some countries the process has involved the central bank taking over banknote issuing not only from commercial banks but also from government itself. Examples include the "Greenbacks" issued by the US Treasury during the Civil War and the "Bradburys" – so-called from the name of the official who signed them – issued by the UK Treasury during the Great War of 1914-1918. The precise arrangements today vary from country to country. In the UK, for example, as in other European countries with feudal traditions, coins are produced by the Royal Mint which comes directly under the Treasury. Banknotes are issued by the Bank of England for England and Wales, but commercial banks in Scotland and Northern Ireland still produce their own. The principle of seigniorage reform is not affected by such variations as these, though they will affect the detailed legislative and administrative changes that will be needed.

2 On the same point, on UK banknotes the Bank of England's Chief Cashier still says "I promise to pay the bearer on demand the sum of...". As long ago as the parliamentary debate on the 1954 Currency and Banknotes Act, this was being ridiculed as meaningless. The idea that money is not actually money but only a promise to pay money, and is therefore a debt, is a good example of the "smoke and mirrors" which characterise the present monetary system. By contrast, US Federal Reserve Notes (dollar bills) state clearly "This note is legal tender for all debts, public and private".

Chapter 4

THE WIDER CASE FOR SEIGNIORAGE REFORM

"The fundamental problem... is to find a social system which is efficient economically and morally."

J.M. Keynes, 1925, unpublished paper quoted by Skidelsky (1992: 241).

4.1 A Principle Of Equity And Justice

In Chapter 2.4 we mentioned the principle that the value of common resources should be shared among all citizens; it should not be 'enclosed' by private interests. In practice this means that monetary values arising from the activities and demands of society at large, or created by the processes of Nature, should be a source of public revenue; whereas monetary values created by the work and skill and enterprise of individuals and businesses should be respected as legitimate private earnings and commercial profit. This principle clearly applies to the value of the new money created and put into circulation as official currency in accordance with the needs of the economy and the objectives of monetary policy. (It also supports the proposal – which is not part of seigniorage reform – for the "tax shift" mentioned in 2.4, away from taxes on employment, incomes, profits and value added, and towards higher taxes or charges on energy, resources, pollution and the site-value of land).

Allowing banks to create new money out of nothing enables them to cream off a special profit. They lend the money to their customers at the full rate of interest, without having to pay any interest on it themselves. So their profit on this part of their business is not, say, 9% credit-interest less 4% debit-interest = 5% normal profit; it is 9% credit-interest less 0% debit-interest = 9% profit = 5% normal profit plus 4% additional special profit. This additional special profit is hidden from bank customers and the public, partly because most people do not know how the system works, and partly because bank balance sheets do not show that some of their loan funding comes from money the banks have created for the purpose and some from already existing money which they have had to borrow at interest.

Our estimate of these annual special profits is as follows: USA about $37bn; Eurozone €58bn; UK £21bn; Germany DM30bn; Japan ¥1,846bn (see Table 4, line B). Excluding the figure for Germany as part of the Eurozone, the total for the four currency areas amounts to about $144bn a year (exchange rates at mid-April, 2000). These special profits differ in amount from the increases in public revenue (see Chapter 2.1) to be expected from seigniorage reform. They reflect the interest on new money now created as bank loans; the additions to public revenue will reflect the quantities of new money that will be created after seigniorage reform.

These special profits represent a sort of private tax – a privileged subsidy in favour of the banks against everyone else. This private levying of tribute is at odds with the constitutional consensus we live in today. It is inequitable. Its social consequences are undesirable. Economically it flouts the principle that participants in an efficient market economy will play on a level field. It is wrong that people, businesses, and governments now have to pay the banks these special profits over and above the normal profit they would expect to pay for goods and services in general. There is no reason of social equity, economic efficiency, or environmental sustainability why governments should allow commercial banks to collect this value as a subsidy. Quite the reverse. It should be collected by the state as public revenue.

In a talk in London in 1999 on land value taxation Professor Mason Gaffney of the University of California referred to the reaction of some right-wing libertarian economists to calls for economic justice. Their response is "TANSTAAFL" (there ain't no such thing as a free lunch). As he pointed out, they are wrong. The truth is TISATAAFL (there is such a thing as a free lunch); and the important questions are WIGI (who is getting it?) and WOTGI (who ought to get it?). Where the issuing of new money is concerned, the answers are: the commercial banks are now getting the free lunch; in future all citizens ought to get their share of it – as public revenue.

4.2 The Social Dimension

When the new seigniorage revenue is spent into circulation by governments, the social impacts of the new money entering the economy will become more heavily influenced by their priorities and less by the priorities of the commercial banks. The general effect of this seems likely to be that a greater proportion of new money than at present will be spent to meet social needs.

More specifically, many advocates of monetary reform (e.g. Rowbotham 1998, Armstrong 1996, Kennedy 1995) argue that issuing an overwhelming proportion of new money as interest-bearing debt has damaging social impacts. One argument, briefly, is that issuing money as debt creates more indebtedness in society than issuing it debt-free will do, and that indebtedness plays a significant part in the creation of poverty and the transfer of wealth from poorer to richer people and poorer to richer countries. Another argument is that creating new money with matching amounts of debt results in the prices of all goods and services being significantly higher than they would be if the money required to produce them and distribute them had been issued debt-free. Issuing it debt-free would reduce prices by eliminating the significant proportion of costs that now arises from the need to pay interest on the original money as it circulates through the economy. Because having to meet that extra cost hits poorer people relatively harder than richer people, the present way of creating new money is socially regressive. So the direct effects of seigniorage reform will be socially beneficial.

One of us, Robertson, accepts that that view seems to make sense. He expects seigniorage reform to make a direct contribution to the amelioration of existing social problems and injustices. He believes that putting new money into circulation debt-free is likely to help to reduce the damaging aspects of indebtedness, including the transfer of wealth from poor to rich and the contribution which that makes to social exclusion.

Huber takes a different view. He sees no reason to accept that creating new money as debt increases the aggregate amount of indebtedness in society or, therefore, that seigniorage reform will reduce it. Demand for borrowing, hence debt, will continue to exist, independently of the mechanism of issuing the money by which a loan is made. Huber sees indebtedness, in the sense of having too many liabilities compared with assets and income, primarily as a question of income distribution. There is lack of income in many places, but no shortage of circulating stock of money. Solutions to the problems of poverty, inequitable income distribution, and social exclusion must be found. But we should not look to a debt-free stock of money for immediate solutions to those problems – although seigniorage reform would help to overcome certain economic distortions, such as excessive public debt, special banking profits, suboptimal investment and employment, which in turn would help to achieve more balanced patterns of allocation and distribution.

This difference is of comparatively little significance. Some supporters of seigniorage reform appear to hope that debt can be eliminated from economic life altogether. We both agree that this is not feasible, or indeed desirable. Borrowing money, and paying and receiving interest on loans, will continue to play a key role in economic life, and banks will continue to develop the credit-broking side of their business. We both agree that seigniorage reform will not necessarily reduce aggregate levels of borrowing and lending. What it will do is leave or channel more debt-free income to firms and households, by making it possible either to reduce taxation and/or government borrowing or to increase public spending. This will encourage a more widely spread build-up of incomes, savings and capital ownership, providing a firmer base of savings and capital for borrowing and lending within sound limits, and indirectly contributing to greater social cohesion in that way.

4.3 The Constitutional Dimension

Over the past century central banks have evolved from private sector institutions to agencies of government – nation-state bodies cooperating internationally. This is a matter of legal fact and practice, even if some traces of their private sector origins remain – e.g. in the USA, where formally the Federal Reserve System is still a private consortium. The Bank of England was nationalised in 1946.

Paradoxically, this evolution has been accompanied in recent decades by a contrary shift of power away from monetary control by government and central bank to private sector financial corporations, encouraged by the effects of cashless payment practices reinforced by technical innovation (electronic money) and globalisation. The time has come to counter this shift, to take the next step in the longer-term trend in the development of central banks from being private sector commercial concerns towards being institutions of public policy, and to transfer full control of the stock of official money to central banks. The national monetary order will then be fully recognised as one aspect of the public order, and the stock of official money as a public domain. The creation and regulation of official money will be accepted as a public policy task, for which a public authority such as a central bank should become fully responsible – on a basis of democratic accountability combined with a high degree of independence (see Chapter 2.5, 2.6).

This will have the important advantage of separating control of how much money is in circulation from decisions on how the money is used. The way commercial banks now create money involves their controlling its use. In deciding whether to grant a loan they exert investment control. But, in a market economy which aspires to be free, open and efficient, decisions affecting the monetary order itself – including the amount of money in circulation – should not be part of the money-making process.

Seigniorage reform will not restrict the freedom of the banks to give and take loans against interest. Far from being a step on the road to any kind of inefficient, centrally planned economy, it will contribute to freer, more open and more efficient functioning of the market economy – for banks as for everyone else. It was Irving Fisher who insisted that the monetary order and the official money of a national economy were questions of constitutional importance. As he put it, "Nationalisation of money, yes; of banking, no" (1935: 58, 241).

4.4 Reducing Inflationary Tendencies

Chapter 2.5 explained why seigniorage reform will make it easier, not more difficult, for central banks to control the monetary causes of inflation. They will be in a position to decide how much new money to put into circulation. This will make it easier for them than it is now to ensure that neither too much nor too little is created, and that will make it easier to avoid excessive inflation or deflation. Other effects of seigniorage reform may also help to reduce inflationary tendencies. Some monetary reformers, particularly in the tradition of C.H. Douglas but others also (e.g. Hixson 1991, 1997), have argued that inflationary tendencies are inevitable in an economy that has to keep prices high enough to cover the interest and repayment costs of money created as interest-bearing debt, especially if the authorities have to use higher interest rates as an instrument of monetary control. Expenditure on interest payments and debt repayments has to come from income derived from the prices of goods and services sold, just as other costs do. If the economy no longer needed to pay interest on and eventually to repay money that had been created as debt, that expenditure would no longer be needed, and prices would therefore come down.

We hesitate, however, to place too much reliance on this as a necessary argument in support of seigniorage reform. Questions about the flexibility and rigidity of prices are complex, and the cost theory of prices is controversial. Although at first sight it may seem likely that a debt-free stock of money will contribute to a lower aggregate level of costs and therefore of prices, we are prepared to accept that this may need study in greater depth.

On the other hand, the debt-free stock of money spent into circulation by government after seigniorage reform will certainly help to create a better balance of supply and demand for capital. By making it possible to reduce taxes and/or government borrowing, or to increase public spending, it will increase the availability of savings for capital investment and enable more people to build up capital of their own. By easing the relative shortage of capital, this will help to move interest rates downward. The connection between interest rates and inflation will help to move inflation downwards too. In short, we conclude it must be accepted that seigniorage reform will create a tendency towards lower levels of interest rates and inflation.

4.5 Greater Economic Stability

When an economic downturn threatens, bank customers try to pay off or at least reduce their existing loans and try to postpone taking out new loans. That has the effect of reducing the money supply, or at least slowing down its growth. That has a further deflationary impact on the economy, and a downward spiral begins to take hold. In extreme cases the downward spiral can turn into a severe depression or slump, leading to drastic falls in employment, sales, profits, investment and the value of assets (like houses). The prospect of an economic upturn puts the process into reverse. People and companies become eager to borrow in order to invest or spend, the renewed borrowing increases the supply of money in circulation, asset values rise, and an upward spiral takes hold. In extreme cases this creates a runaway boom. The "over-heated" economy then has to be cooled by raising interest rates to choke off borrowing and prevent further large increases in the amount of money in circulation.

In these conditions commercial banks, as profit-seeking businesses, naturally behave procyclically, not anticyclically. They expand credit creation in upswings, and reduce it in downswings. The result is that bank-created money positively contributes to overheating and overcooling business cycles, amplifying their peaks and troughs, causing recurrent over- and undershooting of the optimum quantity of money in circulation, and systematically contributing to instability of prices in general and interest rates in particular. So under the present system, positive feedback – generated by the link between the quantity of money in circulation, the demand for loans by bank customers, and the readiness of the banks to supply them – amplifies the volatility of the economy, increasing the scale and accelerating the pace of the swings between highs and lows, peaks and troughs, of the economic cycle.

This has damaging economic and social effects. For example, as many people in the UK experienced in the late 1980s and early 1990s, it can contribute to a dramatic rise in house prices, which both fuels and is fuelled by higher levels of borrowing. This may then be followed by an equally dramatic fall in house prices. And many people may then be trapped in "negative equity" – with debts greater than the reduced value of their houses, with higher rates of interest to pay than when they originally borrowed their house-purchase money, and with significantly worse prospects of keeping their jobs or getting new ones.

It can be argued, of course, that many factors affect the stability of prices and purchasing power, the quantity of money in circulation being just one important factor among them. But the question that concerns us here is simply whether, with regard to that factor, central banks with full control of the stock of money can be expected to exercise monetary control more effectively than at present to deal with fluctuations in the economic cycle. Will they be able to smooth them out more effectively than they can now when new money is created by commercial banks as interest-bearing debt? The answer is obviously Yes.

4.6 Safety and Stability of Money and Banks

As described in Chapter 3, seigniorage reform will mean that money held by bank customers in their sight deposit accounts (i.e. as part of the pool of plain money consisting of sight deposits and cash) will clearly remain their money and not the banks'. The banks will hold it for them as their agents, for safekeeping and as a basis for providing them with cash and payment services. But the banks will not be able to use it for their own business purposes, e.g. in order to lend it to someone else, unless they have explicitly borrowed it from their customers. Borrowing it from their customers will involve transferring the plain money from customers' current accounts to the bank itself, in exchange for equivalent deposits in savings accounts or other similar accounts. Those deposits in savings accounts will not be money itself; they will represent claims on the part of customers to be repaid the money that the bank has borrowed from them.

By disentangling money itself from claims for repayment of money, seigniorage reform will make it easier for the authorities both to ensure the safety of the money belonging to bank customers in their current accounts, and to monitor the safety and stability of the banks' borrowing and lending activities. Today the legal status of sight deposits as merely a liability of the bank to the customer means that, if a bank fails, those deposits are at stake. During the Great Depression many people in America lost all their money that way.

Since then, of course, the situation has changed somewhat. Governments now provide some guarantees for bank deposits, and central banks, as lenders of last resort, are expected to bail out banks in trouble. But providing such a privileged safety net for banks is controversial within an open market system in which conditions should be equal for all. Bailing out banks in trouble privatises profits while shifting risk, loss and debt on to the taxpayer. Moreover, the underlying problem has not been resolved.

Whether bail-outs on a large scale would work in the event of a severe general banking crisis has never been tested.

By contrast, if after seigniorage reform a bank should fail, only the bank's own money will be at stake. Customers' money on current accounts will no longer be part of its balance sheet. Their savings deposits will, of course, continue to be at stake and, as with savings and investments of any kind, customers will have to assess how safe they are likely to be. But disentangling those deposits from money itself will make it easier for the authorities to monitor their safety.

One further point concludes this section. The present UK government has transferred responsibility for the safety and stability of banks and other financial institutions from the Bank of England to the Financial Services Authority (FSA), leaving the Bank to concentrate on monetary policy. This almost appears to match the proposed disentanglement of savings deposits from money held in current accounts. However, to recognise the need for this disentanglement is not to deny the close link between economic stability and the safety and stability of banks and financial institutions. The link was clearly demonstrated by the financial crises that arose in different parts of the world – from Latin America to South East Asia, from Russia to Japan – during the 1980s and 1990s. The framework for co-operation set out in the Memorandum of Understanding between the Treasury, Bank of England and FSA of October 1997 reflects how seriously it is taken (Bank of England 1998a: 37–40).

4.7 Liberating the Real Economy

Special banking profits, seigniorage foregone and high levels of public debt are related to each other. They have a markedly negative effect on the real economy. While they deliver higher interest income to the banking sector and the well-to-do, they restrict general savings and a wider build-up of capital. They cause the general level of interest and other prices to be higher than it would otherwise be. They contribute to a vicious spiral involving higher public subsidies, higher welfare spending, higher taxation, and higher public borrowing – and reducing private and public investment, and opportunities for employment, below what they would otherwise be. Seigniorage reform will help to turn that spiral positive.

Its immediate financial benefit will be to relieve private and public budgets from having to pay for the special banking profits arising from bank-creation of debt-money (Table 4, line B). In addition, governments will have the seigniorage revenue from creating new money (lines I and J). Adding public revenue to the relief from interest (line E) indicates the probable benefit to the real economy from seigniorage reform. It suggests that in the UK it would currently amount to about £66bn a year.

This benefit will go directly or indirectly to people and businesses. They will not have to pay for the interest now arising from newly issued money, or for that part of the tax burden which is replaced with seigniorage. If part of the new seigniorage revenue is used to raise public spending, that will go to people and businesses by a different route. The general level of interest rates and taxes will fall. All in all, the private budgets of households and businesses will benefit significantly.

A debt-free money base, a less indebted government, a better balanced government budget, a lowered tax burden, a better moneyed civil society – all these will contribute to a higher level of net income and a larger capital base for both businesses and private households. This will help to make them less dependent on subsidies and allowances and external capital, and better able to provide for themselves and one another.

In a more specific way, too, seigniorage reform will remove a present cause of economic distortion. As suggested in 4.2, channelling new money into circulation via the banking system as loans to bank customers may have undesirable social effects. The same applies to its economic effects. As Richard Douthwaite puts it (1999, 51), it allows the banks to "shape the way the economy develops. This is because they determine who can borrow, and for what purposes, according to criteria that favour those with a strong cash flow and/or substantial collateral". As a result, the present money system favours the economically strong and rich, and discriminates against smaller firms and poorer individuals. The new non-cash money created today is channelled into activities to which banks and bigger borrowers give priority.

Seigniorage reform will remove the power of the banks to combine issuing new money with deciding how the money is to be used and invested. As powerful brokers of savings and loans they will still be able – other things being equal – to control investment priorities for the money they borrow to lend. However, seigniorage reform could mean that other things will not remain altogether equal. When people can distinguish more clearly between the money they keep for themselves in their current accounts and the money they lend to their bank, they may be more likely to want to influence how the money they lend is channelled into the economy and what purposes it is used for. In other words, seigniorage reform might help to boost "ethical", "green" or "social" banking.

4.8 The Environmental Dimension

Ethical, green and social banking is not the subject of this report. But a discussion of seigniorage reform does have an environmental dimension.

It is argued by some recent writers on monetary reform that the present method of creating new money – "as a money supply system that collapses if it is denied continuous expansion" (Douthwaite 1999: 27) – is incompatible with environmentally sustainable development. A further argument, mentioned in evidence last year to UK parliamentary committees (Robertson 1999), is that, when almost all the money in circulation originates in loans that have to be paid back with interest, the economy is subject to more powerful money-must-grow pressures than it would be if all new money had been put into circulation debt-free. Because extra money has to be earned to pay the interest and repay the debt created simultaneously with the money required to finance the processes of production and distribution, more goods and services must be produced and sold, involving higher levels of resource use and pollution, than would otherwise be necessary. So creating new money as debt is a contributory factor to unsustainable development that seigniorage reform would remove.

The question whether creation of money by interest-bearing loans contributes to existing growth pressures represents an analogy to the question whether it contributes to indebtedness (see 4.2 Social Dimension above). Accordingly, there is the same difference of opinion between us here. Robertson believes that the arguments in the previous paragraph make sense, and that issuing new money as debt almost certainly helps to stimulate unsustainable development.

Huber finds no evidence that it does. He sees no reason why, as a consequence of seigniorage reform, there will be less borrowing and lending. As a consequence, when it comes to the question of how interest payments on loans can be financed, there remains the unhappy choice between inequitable redistribution of income from borrowers to lenders, or the acceptance of what Tobin called a certain "grease rate" level of inflation, or ongoing growth which so far has been ecologically unsustainable. So there remain questions going far beyond the scope of seigniorage reform, which will need different solutions.

However, we both agree that the question whether the money supply will continue to grow indefinitely raises a relevant point. It is sometimes suggested that, in an environmentally sustainable economy, growth of the money supply may have to slow down, then stop, and eventually perhaps go into reverse. That suggestion is linked to the belief that indefinitely continuing economic growth will not be compatible with sustainable development. The rights and wrongs of that controversial issue do not concern us here. The relevant point is a more hypothetical and technical one. If and when a time should come to slow the growth of the money stock, halt it, or even reverse it by withdrawing money from circulation, would seigniorage reform make a difference? Would it make it easier or more difficult to do?

The answer is fairly clear. If it had become an objective of monetary policy, it would be a fairly straightforward task for a central bank to slow and then halt the growth of new money and seigniorage over a period of years, and then to begin cancelling sums (raised by taxation) from the government's operational account. That would be less disruptive than raising interest rates sky-high in an effort to compel the banks, first to slow and halt the growth of their profit-making loans to customers, and then to reduce the total value of their existing loans.

4.9 Transparency and Intelligibility

After seigniorage reform, the official money in circulation in a national economy will all have been issued by its central bank. It will include all the non-cash money in the current accounts managed for people and organisations by banks and in those managed by the central bank for the banks and the government, together with the cash held by everyone. It will be easy to calculate how much of it there is. It will no longer be necessary to juggle with confusing aggregates called M0, M1, M2, M3, M3 extended, M4, and so on. There will be simply the one amount of plain money M. Everyone – and that includes politicians, officials, bankers and monetary experts, as well as a growing number of citizens, bank customers and taxpayers – will understand much better than today how the system works. As befits the citizens of a democracy, they will be better able to evaluate and discuss the monetary and financial policies and policy options presented to them.

So let central banks directly control the quantity of the entire stock of money, let the public purse enjoy full seigniorage, and let the banks continue to develop profit-efficient businesses providing loans on the basis of saved income. The monetary system will be transparent and easy to understand. Money supply will be under effective control. Money will be safe. The purchasing power and foreign exchange value of money will be more stable than today. Last but not least, money will be cheaper to obtain for private households, businesses and governments alike.

Chapter 5

REPLIES TO SUGGESTED OBJECTIONS

"Good reasons must, of force, give place to better".

Shakespeare

5.1 Inflation

The first objection to seigniorage reform from its opponents is usually that allowing a government agency to issue new money will mean greater risk of inflation than allowing commercial banks to go on printing it. Chapter 2 has shown how to safeguard against that risk. Chapter 4 has shown that seigniorage reform is actually likely to reduce inflationary pressure in the economy.

5.2 Nationalisation

Some opponents of seigniorage reform suggest it would amount to nationalising the banks. That is to misunderstand it completely. It will simply recognise official currencies for what they are. The banks will operate freely as profit-making private-sector businesses in more equally competitive financial markets than today.

The possibility that the growth of currencies other than official currencies will continue, and the proposal that currencies should in general be denationalised, are discussed at 5.6 below.

5.3 A Tax on Money

The objection is sometimes heard that collecting the value of newly created money as public revenue will be to put a tax on money. The argument seems to be: first that, if the commercial banks were operating in a highly competitive market, competition between them would compel them to pass on to their customers all of the special profits they now make from issuing new money; and, second, that the effect of this would be to distribute those profits efficiently and fairly throughout society. That argument is questionable on both points. Competition between banks is not sufficiently fierce to achieve the first; and there is no reason to suppose that, even if it was, the resulting distribution of the special profits would be economically efficient and socially fair.

In fact the objection backfires. Defining seigniorage as a tax involves recognising that allowing the commercial banks to create new money, as now, allows them to levy a private tax. Few people would agree that that is preferable to collecting the value of new official money as public revenue.

5.4 Impact on Banking Services and Charges

Banks may object that losing the right to print new money will reduce the quality and increase the costs of their services to their customers.

For example, they may claim that distinguishing more sharply between store-of-value money in savings accounts and means-of-payment money in current accounts will involve a loss of flexibility and a rise in costs for their customers. Customers may have to take more trouble to keep their current accounts in credit and, in order to keep them in credit, they may have to pay more than at present to borrow at short notice, e.g. by overdraft.

It is true that, under today's arrangements, when customers borrow by overdraft their banks create new sight deposits. Seigniorage reform will mean they can no longer provide overdrafts that way. However, bank customers will notice little difference. Banks will have to make some change in their operational procedures. On the basis of past experience and future projections they will have to forecast how much money they will need to meet the demand for overdrafts, and they will have to arrange in advance that the money they need will be immediately available. In principle, this is what they do today, to prevent shortfalls on their balance sheets. In practice, they may have to borrow rather more than they do today, both from their customers as savings deposits and in the money market, and this will reduce profit margins on their overdraft business. But it will still be profitable business.

Today, bank customers pay interest of 12–16% on overdrafts which cost the banks virtually nothing. If banks have to pay 4–6% interest for borrowing the money, they will still make a decent profit. Overdrafts illustrate how seigniorage reform will cut excess banking profits and encourage banking to seek its profits more competitively.

Banks may also claim that, to compensate for their loss of special profits after seigniorage reform, they will have to raise charges for managing current accounts, carrying out cashless payments, and providing cash facilities. Although there may be differences between different countries in this respect – for example, more German banks than UK banks probably now charge service fees that cover costs – nonetheless, all banks may be tempted to try to recoup their loss of special seigniorage profits by increasing charges to customers.

This will call further attention to the question of regulating bank competitiveness and profitability, discussed in the recent Cruickshank Report in the UK. Other competitive pressures, such as the growth of internet banking, may also help to keep charges down. Moreover, seigniorage reform may strengthen the tendency to split investment banking from the management of accounts. The question may even arise whether, as Goodhart argues in the context of banking safety (1989: 181ff), "it would be perfectly possible (and generally safer) for transactions services to be provided by an altogether different set of financial intermediaries". All in all, we see little reason to fear that seigniorage reform will seriously affect the quality and cost of payments services available to bank customers.

5.5 Possible Loopholes: Minimum Notice Policy

After seigniorage reform it will be illegal for banks to create non-cash money denominated in the official currency. Credit broking will be permissible, credit creation will not – and will not be feasible. When credit is supplied it will have to come out of existing money already belonging to the lender or borrowed from someone else, and not be new money created by the act of lending it. To create new money and put it into circulation will be treated as counterfeiting or forgery. But – the objection is heard – how are banks to be prevented from breaking or evading the law in this respect?

With regard to breaking the law, the reply is a series of questions. How at present are banks and anyone else prevented from counterfeiting coins and banknotes? Or breaking existing banking law in other ways? Why, after seigniorage reform, should measures to enforce the new banking law prohibiting the creation of non-cash money be less effective than measures to enforce the law governing monetary and banking activities today? But with regard to evading, as opposed to breaking, the law, the reply is not quite so straightforward. For example, do credit cards not create credit? Are they to be prohibited? And will commercial banks and other financial institutions not be able to invent legal ways round the prohibition to create new money?

The answer about credit cards is, in fact, No, they do not create new money. Of course credit card companies lend money to users of their cards. But they finance it:

▶ by spreading the monthly timing of their customers' payments of bills so as to minimise the total amount by which the money the companies pay to the sellers of items purchased by their cards ever exceeds their receipts from their customers,

▶ charging the sellers of items purchased by their cards a percentage of the price,

▶ by charging interest to card users who do not pay off their debts immediately, and

▶ when necessary, by short-term overdrafts from their bank just like other bank customers.

When card users pay for their purchases, they pay with sight deposits from their current accounts. In order to pay, they may need to borrow from their bank and thereby actuate the creation of new money by the bank. But it will be created by their bank, not by the credit card company. Seigniorage reform should have no impact on credit card users or credit card companies.

Banks might perhaps try to create loopholes and evade the consequences of seigniorage reform in the two following ways. But these could be frustrated by central banks, if they did not simply fail.

First, banks might try to replace their use of today's current-account system to create credit, by arranging very short-term borrowing at low interest from their customers. They would obtain permission to withdraw money from their customers' current accounts whenever there was money in them, on the understanding that the bank would pay back instantly to the customer any sum on demand. This would not increase the quantity of plain money in circulation, but eventually it might risk increasing the velocity of its circulation to a point that would jeopardise the effectiveness of monetary control.

In that case very short-term borrowing between banks and the public might need to be prohibited. This might involve setting a minimum notice for withdrawing money lent by the public to a bank, on the lines of the customary notice for withdrawing time deposits on which many banks still insist. Minimum notice policy might even come to be used by the central bank as a new instrument of monetary control, directed at the velocity of money instead of its quantity or price. It would affect the velocity of financial circulation only, not real economic circulation. It would replace the traditional instrument of minimum reserves – obsolete once seigniorage reform had changed sight deposits into actual non-cash money.

On the inter-bank money market, in contrast to high-street banking, very short-term borrowing is already business-as-usual. There are weekly rates, 2-day-rates, overnight rates, and – who knows – perhaps hourly rates will become common in the future. So, in its use of the new policy instrument, the central bank would apply different periods of minimum notice to interbank dealings, from those it applied to dealings between banks and their customers – say, 3 or 10 days in inter-bank circulation and 20, 40 or 60 or more days between banks and their customers. Insofar as this slowed down the velocity of money circulating in financial transfers, the central bank would have to create a correspondingly larger stock of money.

This would do no harm at all. There would be no money shortage or capital shortage. Real-economic transactions and monetary transfers other than the very short-term would continue as if nothing had changed. There would be no inflationary impact. Neither more nor less money would be spent than would have been spent otherwise. The difference would simply be that more non-cash money would stay unused in current accounts, just as some of the cash in one's pocket or wallet may stay unused for several days or even weeks.

The second possibility is that a bank might persuade its customers to open, say, 'easy accounts' with 'virtual deposits' denominated in a new unofficial currency belonging to the bank itself, but linked in value to the official currency. It would not be illegal to do this and to create credit in the new private currency, unless the law prohibited transactional payments not made with legal tender. But nevertheless the scheme would be unlikely to succeed. Unless large numbers of people were already using these accounts – both as payers and receivers – in parallel with their plain money current accounts, it would not be worth joining it. Under normal conditions, legal tender is always preferred to unofficial money – as the theory of chartal money predicts (Knapp 1905, Keynes 1930). This can be seen, for example, when Eurocheques are not accepted by third parties in place of legal tender banknotes.

5.6 Parallel and Unofficial Currencies

This objection suggests that seigniorage reform is a low priority, even a distraction; what is needed is greater monetary pluralism; the age of "one country, one currency" is past. So why spend time and effort changing the way new official money is now created?

For example, the US dollar is now used in many countries for internal transactions as a parallel currency alongside their own national currencies. Many non-American companies use it in international trade, and many non-American individuals use it for international travel. Even if the UK does not become part of the Eurozone, UK companies and citizens could increasingly find themselves using the euro as a parallel currency, especially but not only for transactions with Eurozone countries. Then there is the increasing use of non-official currencies, quasi-currencies and vouchers, initiated by businesses and communities. Business examples include *Wir* (the currency of a co-operating group of Swiss businesses). Community examples include several hundred LETS (local exchange trading systems) and similar schemes like Time Dollars and Ithaca Hours (Boyle 1999, Douthwaite 1999).

There are, broadly, two views on this question. One sees the development of alternative community currencies as temporary self-help initiatives in response to times of economic crisis, as in the 1930s and at present, when increasing numbers of people are unable to earn enough national money to support exchanges of goods and services among themselves in their own localities.

The other view is that, in a globalised economy, there will be a permanent need for community currencies and other local currencies, which should therefore be encouraged. Sizeable nations and multinational currency unions are bound to contain areas that will suffer from the one-size-fits-all monetary policy that goes with a single currency. Nor need there be objection to private sector special-purpose currencies like *Wir* or voucher/quasi-currencies like Air Miles. Even proprietary currencies issued into general circulation by commercial banks as proposed by Hayek (see below) might not necessarily have to be ruled out on principle, if there were a demand for them, if their users were informed of their risks, if it were clear that their value was not guaranteed by the state, and if they were subject to fair trading regulations.

Debate between these two views throws up important and interesting questions, which should certainly be further studied and discussed. But we do not need to pursue them here. Whichever of the two views is taken, for practical purposes official currencies like the dollar, the euro, the pound and the yen will obviously continue to play a dominant role in economic life for many years to come. It cannot be seriously argued that the expansion of parallel (or "alternative" or "complementary") currencies will so reduce the ability of governments to control the amount of purchasing power in the economy that proposals to change the method of issuing official money are out-of-date. The growing interest in 'funny money' is not an argument against seigniorage reform.

More far-reaching is the proposal to denationalise money (Hayek 1976: 22–30). This is based on the view that "history is largely a history of inflation, and usually of inflations engineered by governments and for the gain of governments", and that for the future it will continue to be politically impossible for "any democratic government with unlimited powers" to resist pressures to inflate the currency and manage the money supply with sufficient discipline to keep the currency stable. That does not mean, however, that it is technically impossible to control the quantity of money so that the currency will retain its acceptability and value.

Hayek's proposed remedy, therefore, is to abolish "government monopoly of the provision of money" and throw it open to "the competition of private concerns supplying different currencies... clearly distinguishable by different denominations among which the public could choose freely". There will then be no need to rely on the benevolence and self-discipline of governments to provide good money, but on the regard of the banks for their own commercial interests.

This proposal does not, in fact, constitute a significant practical objection to seigniorage reform. It is unlikely to be accepted for many years, if ever, that private commercial currencies should be encouraged to replace official currencies. Even when it had been accepted, if ever, many more years would pass before official currencies would actually have been phased out and replaced by the new commercial currencies. So, for practical purposes, it would be absurd to suggest that a proposal to change the existing method of creating official money has been outdated by the proposal to denationalise money. Moreover, the most important argument for denationalising money, that political governments must be prevented from debauching the currency, is given top priority by the institutional arrangements that must be a key aspect of seigniorage reform – to ensure that the amounts of new money to be put into circulation are openly decided by central monetary authorities with a high degree of independence from politicians and the political arms of government.

Finally, although – for the reasons just given – it is not necessary to consider here in detail the practical and theoretical merits and demerits of the idea of denationalising currencies, a few questions will suggest that it would indeed take a long time to get it accepted. Is it likely that a significant number of stable currencies issued by a significant number of competing currency suppliers could circulate through an economy under stable conditions of fair competition? What would ensure that commercial currencies were no more volatile than an official currency, but were as safe and stable? What measures, including effective government regulation, would be necessary to counteract possible tendencies for the monetary system to decline either into commercial monopoly or into commercial anarchy? What would prevent currency speculation becoming a feature of the domestic economy, with people switching into currencies expected to revalue and out of currencies expected to devalue? When a bank and its currency failed, would there be any lender of last resort or any state guarantee of deposits in current or savings accounts?

It seems quite clear that, for practical purposes, the proposal to denationalise money provides no stronger an argument against going ahead with seigniorage reform, than does the growth of local community currencies.

5.7 Electronic Money

Another suggestion that seigniorage reform may be an out-of-date proposition is based on the prospect that new account facilities offering payments management services will develop on the internet, in step with the growth of electronic commerce (internet trading), electronic money transmission, and portable electronic money storage (as in electronic smart cards or "e-purses"). The suggestion is that the providers of those facilities, who will not necessarily be banks, will be in a position to offer their customers credit which they will be able to create much as the banks now do, and that central banks will find it very difficult to supervise these credit creation activities on the internet and exercise monetary control over them.

Much current discussion focuses on the need for a regulatory framework which, according to Birch 1999, will include "measuring and controlling the money supply as the existing flow of legal tender is joined by a stream of e-cash", and about "securing public trust in e-cash issuers who can be banked on (in every sense)". Answers to the questions "What does e-cash supply mean for the overall money supply and for inflation control?" and "Who should be allowed to issue e-cash?", have so far reflected "two broad camps: those who think that e-cash should be issued by banks or non-bank financial institutions only, and those who think that e-cash could be issued by anyone". The possibility that seigniorage reform might help to provide an answer to the problem has not been seriously considered.

A far-reaching possibility for the future was outlined by one of the Bank of England's Deputy Governors, Mervyn King, in a speech last year at an international conference of central bankers. He suggested that electronic transactions in real time hold out the possibility that one day it will be possible for final settlements to be carried out by the private sector without the need for clearing through the central bank. Although this would need much greater computing power than is at present available, there is no conceptual reason to prevent two individuals settling a transaction by a transfer of wealth from one electronic account to another in real time. The assets transferred could be any financial assets for which market-clearing prices were available in real time. Financial assets and real goods and services would still have to be priced in terms of a unit of account. But a single process could simultaneously match demands and supplies of financial assets, determine prices and make settlements.

At present, central banks are the monopoly supplier of base money – cash and bank reserves (bankers' operational deposits). Because base money is the ultimate medium of exchange and of final settlement, this gives central banks leverage over the value of transactions in the economy. That is the key to a central bank's ability to implement monetary policy. Without such a role in settlements, central banks would no longer exist in their present form; nor would money. The need to limit excessive money creation would be replaced by a concern to ensure the integrity of the computer systems used for settlement purposes, and the integrity of the unit of account. A regulatory body would be required, which would operate along the lines of existing weights and measures inspectors. Existing regulators, including central banks, would no doubt compete for that responsibility. But there would no longer be a unique role for base money. "The successors to Bill Gates would have put the successors to Alan Greenspan out of business" (King 1999).

Two comments are relevant.

First, is a monetary unit of account, which is a unit of value, comparable to a unit of weight or length? A monetary unit like a dollar or a euro or a pound can change in value in a way that an inch or a metre, or an ounce or a kilogram, cannot change in length or weight. No controversies arise about the supply of metres or kilograms – have too many or too few been put into circulation? The practical task of ensuring that a monetary unit of account maintains a stable value is a different kind of task from inspection to prevent people deceiving one another about the characteristics and qualities of the goods and services they offer for sale. To ensure that a unit of account maintains a stable value will surely always be important, and it will surely always require – among other things – action to regulate the combined effect on purchasing power of the quantity of units of account in circulation and the velocity with which they circulate.

Second, after seigniorage reform, it will no longer be the case that the capacity of central banks to implement monetary policy will depend on their role as monopoly supplier of cash and bank reserves as the ultimate medium of exchange in final settlement. After seigniorage reform, central banks will exercise monetary control by directly regulating the quantity of units of account available for transaction purposes, taking into consideration a range of relevant factors including the velocity of their financial circulation – which, incidentally, seigniorage reform may have tended to reduce in some degree (see 5.5 above).

How monetary control can be effectively implemented in a world in which money is turning into electronic information capable of almost instantaneous transmission and almost instantaneous processing in increasingly complex ways, is a crucially important and urgent subject for study. But it appears that, so far from electronic money having reduced the relevance of seigniorage reform, it has increased it. Seigniorage reform appears much more likely to offer a solution to the problems raised by electronic money than the present methods of monetary control based on the need to regulate indirectly the creation of new money by commercial banks. The authorities should examine this urgently.

5.8 Summing Up the Risks of Evasion

The last three sections have shown, we believe, that sight deposits in current accounts denominated in official currencies are likely to continue to provide the source and destination for the great majority of payment transactions in the world for many years to come. It will be a long time before the need to manage and control the creation of new official money could eventually disappear from the scene. Central banks, with public policy objectives, will continue to be responsible for that function.

Innovations in the monetary, banking and financial system will continue to affect how money is used, the demand for it, and its velocity. Monetary policy, directly based on controlling increases in the amount of money issued into circulation, will require understanding of these changes and their consequences – but no more so than if regulation continues to be based on control of interest rates as it is today. In fact, in the evolving conditions of the Information Age, there is absolutely no reason to suppose that seigniorage reform will increase the opportunities for banks and others to bypass monetary controls. On the contrary, there are convincing arguments for supposing that it will make it easier for the authorities to enforce them.

5.9 Supposed International Disadvantages

Seigniorage reform will probably have to be initiated by one country acting alone. To try to get a number of important countries to introduce it simultaneously would probably run into insuperable inertia and opposition. But will it have damaging international consequences for a country that pioneers it?

Might it cause difficulties for its citizens and businesses engaging in payments transactions with other countries? Might it reduce their flexibility to operate in the foreign exchange markets? Might it have adverse effects on the exchange rate? Might it encourage capital flight? Might depriving that country's banks of the subsidy which they now enjoy from their right to create new money put them at a competitive disadvantage against the still subsidised banks of other countries? Opponents of seigniorage reform may be expected to say that the answer to these questions is Yes. In fact, the answer is No.

A debt-free stock of money will be used by the public at home and abroad in just the same ways as they use money now. Foreign business and trading partners, just like the banks' own customers, would not realise that a seigniorage reform had happened if nobody told them about it. They will find their everyday economic and financial routines undisturbed. Free international convertibility of the currency will not be affected. There will be no bureaucratic control of foreign trade, foreign exchange, or foreign capital transfers. Seigniorage reform will be completely in tune with open international markets and free trade, if those are what governments and people want.

There is no reason to fear a flight of capital from an economy pioneering seigniorage reform. Inflation in the domestic economy will be easier to keep under control. Interest rates will go somewhat lower. The economy will be more stable. Stable prices in a stable economy with interest rates at a lower level will stabilise the foreign exchange value of the currency. That will attract foreign capital to invest in the real economy. An initial fall in interest rates following seigniorage reform might make the national currency less attractive to mobile ("footloose") finance capital, thereby reducing the currency's foreign exchange value. But lower interest rates and a lower foreign exchange rate are not necessarily bad things. For the past few years UK manufacturing industry has been crying out for a lower exchange rate; and Switzerland, with very low interest rates and a relatively stable foreign exchange rate, does not find it difficult to attract foreign capital. At least in the medium and longer term, enhanced economic stability, safe money, stabilised price levels and stable exchange rates will be likely to become more attractive to domestic and inward investment capital, not less.

As regards the argument for continuing to subsidise the banks, we have shown that foregoing seigniorage as public revenue and diverting it to the banks involves heavy costs to public finance and the real economy. There is no evidence that those costs are justified by the support they give to the international competitiveness of a country's banks, and by any additional contribution banks are thereby able to make to national economic performance.

5.10 Towards International Monetary Reform

We conclude this chapter on a positive point, which may be seen as speculative. Its purpose is not to put forward a worked out proposal, but to illustrate the contribution that seigniorage reform might be able to make in the context of international monetary reform.

First, as seigniorage reform is adopted by more and more countries at the national level, more and more national central banks will be in a stronger position to monitor and regulate the financial stability of their banking industries. Co-operation between them will then make it easier to prevent the kind of banking and financial bubble that burst in Asia in the late 1990s.

Second, it seems likely that pressure will grow for the development of global arrangements to meet the monetary needs of a globalised economy. As the independent international Commission on Global Governance pointed out (Commission on Global Governance 1995: 180-188), "the IMF's reserve currency – Special Drawing Rights (SDRs) – currently accounts for only a very minor part of world liquidity". The Commission suggested that the effectiveness and credibility of the IMF "would be enhanced by increasing the issue of SDRs. A growing world economy requires constant enlargement of international liquidity". Among the weaknesses it identified in the current international monetary system were:

▶ "the underlying asymmetry between countries that can maintain adequate liquidity (or solvency) only by borrowing from the IMF – since they have lost, or never gained, access to private capital markets – and countries that have no need of Fund financing";

▶ the United States' "unique luxury of being able to borrow in its own currency abroad and then devalue its repayment obligations"; and

▶ the fact that "the international monetary system's dependence on private capital markets exposes it to the risk of a collapse of confidence in the system as a whole".

If and when the time comes to make arrangements for the more regular enlargement of international liquidity, SDRs might develop into a kind of global quasi-currency to meet that need. Initially it might supplement the US dollar and other national currencies in their global role. As time passed, it might increasingly replace them in that role.

One possibility might be that, following the model of seigniorage reform, money denominated in SDRs would be issued – perhaps by a new international agency combining some of the functions of the IMF and the Bank for International Settlements – into an operational account which it would hold for the United Nations. The UN would spend this money into circulation, partly as a contribution to financing its own operations, and partly – perhaps – as a distribution (based on the size of national populations) to national governments.

This new international agency, which might in due course come to be regarded as an embryonic world central bank, would have to combine accountability with a high degree of independence in its decisions about how much new international liquidity to create. It might perhaps agree the broad terms of its mission with a UN policy-making body accountable to member governments, as a published framework within which to carry out its responsibility for global monetary policy. It might report and be accountable for its performance either to that UN body or to another, such as a committee of the General Assembly.

We shall not go further into this here. We simply wish to note that the model of seigniorage reform at national level could perhaps be relevant to international monetary reform.

Chapter 6

PROSPECTS

"There is nothing more difficult to execute, nor more dubious of success, nor more dangerous to administer, than to introduce a new order of things; for he who introduces it has all those who profit from the old order as his enemies, and he has only lukewarm allies in all those who might profit from the new. This lukewarmness partly stems from fear of their adversaries,.. and partly from the scepticism of men, who do not truly believe in new things unless they have actually had personal experience of them."

Machiavelli, *The Prince*, 1532

Seigniorage reform will provide a classic case study for future students of the statics and dynamics of political and economic change. It will have deprived one of society's most powerful interest groups of the "free lunch" which it enjoyed for centuries, and it will have brought very significant benefits to society as a whole. Over a long period of years the potential losers from the reform will have hotly opposed it.[1] Meanwhile, the much greater numbers of potential beneficiaries will have been lukewarm in their support. What will it have been that eventually made the difference and brought it about?

As Tom Paine said, "There never was any truth or principle so irresistibly obvious that all men believed it at once". We hope we have set out very clearly the irresistibly obvious case for seigniorage reform. But we are not so naive as to suppose that, having done so, we will convert everyone into ardent believers. At the same time, we are not so cynical as to doubt that many people are moved by concern for the common good, and will want to help to achieve the contribution that seigniorage reform can make to it.

A realistic approach must take account of those two angles. It must involve identifying potential opponents and supporters; and then exploring how the opposition of opponents might be reduced and neutralised, and the numbers and commitment of supporters might be increased and strengthened. At present, if they thought about it at all, many potential supporters would probably still conclude it was not worth their while to become actively engaged in seigniorage reform. They would perceive the balance of risk and reward as unfavourable, in terms of their personal priorities, career prospects and alternative ways to spend their energies. If seigniorage reform is to be successfully achieved, it will be because a bandwagon of support begins to roll. More and more people will begin to perceive that the balance of risk and reward is changing, and that supporting the reform is becoming worth their while. How can the bandwagon be set rolling? And how can it gather unstoppable momentum?

6.1 Potential Opponents

The principal opponents of seigniorage reform will come from the commercial banks; their directors, managers and staff; their shareholders; their suppliers; and other beneficiaries. Some of their most important suppliers and beneficiaries include professionals like City accountants and lawyers, and businesspeople trading in up-market goods and services. Many of them will no doubt actively support the banks' opposition.

However, it is important to stress that, although banks will lose today's supernormal profits from the creation of sight deposits in current accounts, the normal profitability of banking business will remain untouched. Banks will be able without any restrictions to continue to carry out every kind of business they do now, e.g. managing deposits and transfers of their clients, granting loans to whomsoever they consider creditworthy, investing in financial assets such as bonds or equity shares for their clients and for themselves, and offering a wide variety of financial products and services. Once bankers and their associates begin to come to terms with the prospect of seigniorage reform, they will start thinking about the new challenges and opportunities the change will present to adaptable and able people in banking and the professions which support it.

Among other financial professionals, commentators and academics with a stake in the present way the banking system works there will probably be some opponents. They will have built up an understanding of the details and complexities of a monetary and banking system founded on bank creation of credit. They will fear that their expertise may lose value and their prospects may suffer if the system is changed. The NIH (not-invented-here) syndrome will result in some being unenthusiastic or even resentful about the seigniorage reform idea, even if they do not have a direct stake in the continuance of the special bank profits due to bank-created credit. They may feel uneasy at the prospect of an idea proving to be a winner, to which in all their years of advising, commentating, studying and teaching, they have paid no attention. Older people may be more affected this way than younger people, who may find it easier to see that the prospect of change offers new opportunities.

Similar reasons to oppose seigniorage reform are likely to apply to some politicians and other influential people. They may have friendly associations with the banks. Or they may fear that, if seigniorage reform turns out to be successful, their failure to have taken an interest in it will be held against them.

6.2 Potential Beneficiaries

As previous chapters have made clear, almost all sectors of society, and the economy as a whole, will benefit from seigniorage reform. There is a large potential reservoir of support for it there. But how will the potential be actualised?

Among direct beneficiaries will be monetary and financial institutions which compete with the banks as financial intermediaries. The banks will no longer have a competitive advantage against them, arising from the subsidy they now get from creating new money.

Central bankers will also be direct beneficiaries – even if some of them may be temperamentally wary about change and prefer to stick to the status quo. They will take over the function of money creation from the commercial banks, and they will consolidate their independent responsibility for the whole of the official money stock. Their role in the further development and reform of the monetary and financial system, domestically and internationally, will be enhanced.

There will also be new career opportunities for other financial regulators, such as those in the Financial Services Authority in the UK, and for ambitious and able lawyers and accountants who become involved in making the new system work.

Academic economists will be in a similar situation. Although opposition may come from some of the older and more established monetary economists on the "can't-teach-old-dogs-new-tricks" principle, growing interest in seigniorage reform will open up a new range of questions and career opportunities for more innovative practitioners of the discipline. It will create new openings in the economics departments of universities and in research institutes in economic and political fields.

For politicians, as Chapter 2 made clear, seigniorage reform will offer opportunities for reducing taxes and public borrowing or for increasing public spending, according to their political persuasion. In terms of personal political career prospects, they will have to think about whether, and if so when, it will be best to express an interest in it and and come out in support for it.

Growing numbers of people active in non-governmental organisations (NGOs), like the churches and the pressure groups concerned with issues of poverty and social exclusion, globalisation, the environment, and economic justice for poorer countries, will realise that seigniorage reform may be an important campaigning issue for them, and that – directly or indirectly – the present failure to create new money debt-free and to spend it into circulation via public spending programmes may have an adverse effect in their particular sphere of concern. Sooner or later a growing number of NGOs may decide to join one another in a coalition of support for seigniorage reform.

6.3 Trigger Issues and Events

Whether for politicians, central bankers, public finance officials, people connected with non-bank financial institutions, financial and economic journalists and commentators, professionals like banking lawyers and accountants, influential people in NGOs, academic economists, and the whole wide range of individuals who are concerned to improve the workings of society and the economy – in almost every case, particular issues and events could help to trigger more active support for seigniorage reform. Here are three examples.

One concerns the European Union (EU). For the governments and parliaments of Eurozone countries, and for the European Parliament too, seigniorage reform could have an immediate significance. It could bring to an end the recurring disputes about national contributions to the EU budget, and it could meet the longstanding wish of EU institutions to have an undisputed European source of revenue of their own. Seigniorage reform could make it possible to do away altogether with national contributions to the EU budget, and – in addition to that – actually enable Brussels to transfer a sizeable seigniorage dividend to Eurozone member states. This might not put an end to all the arguments. But the debate on sharing tax burdens would be turned into a debate on sharing seigniorage revenue. Its starting point could be the formula for distributing shares in the capital of the European Central bank among Eurozone member states (see Chapter 2.1). And its outcome could probably be decided more amicably than arguments about contributions to the European budget today.

The EU budget was €83bn in 1998 and €86bn in 1999, including the opt-out countries. The increase in the stock of money within the Euro area, not including the opt-out countries, was about €185–190bn in 1999 (ECB Monthly Bulletins, Table 2.4). So the EU budget could be more than fully financed by EU seigniorage. On the basis of those figures, national governments of the Eurozone states would be able to stop paying contributions to the EU budget altogether, and – on top of that – actually receive from Brussels more than the amounts they were previously having to pay.

If the Eurozone states decided to introduce seigniorage reform, and the opt-out members of the EU did not, the opt-out states would obviously feel at a disadvantage. Would they feel urged to join EMU? No, not necessarily. But they would certainly feel urged to adopt seigniorage reform themselves. This is a practical example of the bandwagon or domino effect that will mark the progress of seigniorage reform: once one government among economically interdependent states has taken the step, the other governments will feel pressure to follow suit. The successful pioneers will win seigniorage as an extra profit, and the reluctant late-comers will have to adapt. The advantage-and-imitation effect of seigniorage reform will become very clear, especially in the context of the EU. The Eurozone member states can, of course, no longer go it alone in adopting seigniorage reform. By contrast, the Eurozone opt-out states, including the UK, Sweden, and Denmark, can do so without running very much risk of losing their right to opt in at a later date if they wanted to.

Another example might be rising controversy in the UK about Public Private Partnership (PPP) proposals. For example, the government is currently proposing that, in return for a 30-year income stream, private sector operators should contribute £7bn of the investment needed to modernise the London Underground. Critics calculate that, to cover the additional cost compared to the government simply borrowing the £7bn, this would require a 30% rise in fares. This has been a controversial question in the campaign for the election of a Mayor of London in May. Over the next few years, PPP proposals may provide opportunities for getting the message across that, in some cases, seigniorage reform might give taxpayers and consumers a better deal than either PPP or government-issued interest-bearing bonds – regardless of whether the services to be provided will be delivered by the private or the public sector.

A third example could be controversy, as currently in the UK, about the closure of branch banks in rural areas. People may become readier to accept that, as competitive commercial concerns, banks should no longer be expected to provide a public service. But at the same time they are likely to become less ready to accept that banks should continue to receive subsidies of £ billions a year from special banking profits.

As a campaign for seigniorage reform begins to build up, it will be possible to identify many such opportunities for mobilising support.

6.4 Which Countries Could Take The Lead?

Any sovereign country with stable institutions, reasonably reliable government, a sound economy, a respected convertible currency, and a central bank of high standing could pioneer seigniorage reform. So the most obvious candidates are among OECD countries, perhaps especially the United States, the Euro area, or Japan, with the biggest world reserve currencies. The UK, Sweden, Denmark, Switzerland, Canada, New Zealand, and Australia would certainly also be well suited.

Could other countries – such as Russia, China, India, Indonesia, or Brazil – with important domestic economies and important stocks of money denominated in national currency, also undertake seigniorage reform and benefit from it? The answer is, Yes, in principle, but under certain preconditions. These are stable government, rule of law (national and international), non-corrupt public administration, and free convertibility of foreign exchange and domestic currency. Foreign debt would not be a hindrance. Introducing full seigniorage with a convertible currency would create greater confidence that foreign debts would be serviced and repaid.

6.5 Why Now?

It may be asked why seigniorage reform may now be successfully achieved, when the hopes of great men in the past two hundred years – including Jefferson, Lincoln and Gladstone – that the state could recover the exclusive prerogative of creating official money, have failed. There are a number of reasons.

First, there are many more people in the world today than there were even fifty years ago who realise that formal institutions of democracy, which merely allow people to vote for political leaders every few years, are not enough. Economic and financial institutions are also needed which, by predistributing (rather than redistributing) resources more efficiently and fairly, will enable and encourage people to take greater control of their lives and greater responsibility for themselves and others. This is becoming more widely understood.

Second, the impacts of globalisation are radicalising increasing numbers of people in rich and poor countries alike. Economic and financial life is increasingly perceived to be systematically skewed in favour of a privileged minority, within and between countries. Pressures are rising for changes in existing monetary and financial practices and institutions, national and international.

Third, with the arrival of the Information Age, awareness is spreading that the monetary system has become essentially an information system. This is bringing new perspectives and new participants into discussion and debate about how a 21st-century monetary system should be organised and operated.

Fourth, there is the increasingly important environmental factor. Rightly or wrongly, many people see today's monetary and financial system as actively supporting environmentally damaging economic activities. They are increasingly seeking ways to change this.

Hitherto, the relevance of seigniorage reform to these issues has been hidden – concealed by the 'smoke and mirrors' which have been a feature of the monetary and banking system. But that is already beginning to change. As increasing numbers of people in many countries commit themselves to learning more about how money and banks function today and how they could function better, the pressures for seigniorage reform will continue to grow stronger.

6.6 Constituencies For Change

We hope to see a growing number of national and international programmes and campaigns, linked to one another by the internet and using it to spread awareness of the case for seigniorage reform and to mobilise support for it.

They should address the concerns of a range of different groups. Even though the agendas of these groups may be different, each can influence the attitude of the others favourably or unfavourably towards reform. They are as follows:

- politicians and public officials, not necessarily connected with banking and financial affairs;

- the banking industry itself, the central banks, and other national and international monetary and banking institutions;

- the mainstream community of economic and financial policy-makers, policy-analysts, policy-debaters and policy-commentators;

▶ the community of respected monetary academics, monetary historians and other specialist monetary and banking experts;

▶ the wider community of individuals, NGOs and pressure groups, who support proposals for greater economic efficiency and a fairer sharing of resources, but who may as yet be unfamiliar with the relevance of monetary reform; and

▶ the community of already committed supporters of monetary reform.

We hope that our report will attract interest and support from experts and professionals. But it is often difficult for people pursuing a professional career in a particular walk of life to take a positive interest in proposals for its reform until there is widespread recognition that they should. We suggest, therefore, that bodies like the New Economics Foundation should give high priority to spreading awareness of the case for seigniorage reform among politicians and public officials and potentially interested individuals, NGOs and pressure groups. They, together with existing supporters of monetary reform, can then help to create a climate of informed opinion that will make it easier – indeed more compelling – for the experts to give it the serious attention it demands.

Endnotes

1   For example, according to C.H. Douglas, in Britain in the 1920s the Institute of Bankers was allocated £5 million to combat his proposals – *The New Age*, 28th March, 1928.

Appendix

THE STOCK OF MONEY, TODAY AND AFTER SEIGNIORAGE REFORM

Which of the wide range of categories of money defined in existing monetary statistics should be regarded as belonging to the circulating stock of money? How much money exists today, and how much would exist after seigniorage reform? How much is the average annual growth of the stock of money, and how much seigniorage revenue can be expected from it?

In the context of seigniorage reform, these are questions which require answers. This Appendix, supported by the definitions and statistics in Tables 1–4, aims to give them.

A.1 Defining and Measuring Today's Money Stock

Our understanding of the stock of money comes close to the notion of "means of payment". Means of payment should not, of course, be confused with methods of payment or technical aids to payment such as cheques, credit cards, etc. These documents or methods of payment just represent orders for drawing on money which exists in current accounts. They represent a claim to be paid money or a liability to pay money rather than being themselves a means of payment in the sense of money itself.

To most people today the obvious types of money are still coins and banknotes. But it is possible to imagine that within a generation or so the use of cash may be almost completely replaced by "electronic cash", i.e. "bits" carried around on microchips or magnetic strips on plastic cards, and by instant transfer of funds remotely transmitted from one bank account to another with the help of "smart cards" and similar devices.

Our present situation can already be seen as a transitional stage to such a completely non-cash money future. In former times, cash meant coins made of gold and silver, the minor ones of copper. Today, the coins in circulation are made of non-precious metal alloys; banknotes, in wider circulation for the past 300 years, are made of paper; and the Mint could easily decide to produce plastic coin.

It is apparent from this that even cash has a "non-cash" nature. Detached step by step from material things of value, money has disclosed its purely informational nature. The units of money in circulation represent economic value. Money can be related to any item subject to economic valuation (pricing) and transaction (exchange). Hence the dual economic function of money: as units of account, the units of money can serve for counting or measuring economic value; and, as means of payment, they can serve for carrying out transactions by transferring units of money in exchange for items bought. What is usually thought of as their third function – as a "store of value" – refers to the fact that they can be saved as means of payment for use at a later date.

Seen like this, money is a functional tool consisting of value- informational units with a general capacity to match the values of all kinds of goods and services in the real world. It is increasingly questionable whether money can still be regarded as the same kind of store of value as gold, diamonds and other precious stones and metals which were the treasures of former times. Money may help to represent value, but it does not have intrinsic value of its own. We hesitate to say money is worthless or without value, because money gives purchasing power. That purchasing power, however, is not an immanent property of money; it relates to prices of goods, services, labour or capital of any kind.

Purchasing power is directly linked to the prices which are paid with money. "Stable currency" or "stable money" would be meaningless terms unless they referred to stable prices. Prices express the economic value of tangibles and intangibles of any kind. The question where the value of these things comes from, how it is determined by whom, remains unsettled. William Petty laid the foundations of labour theory of value by saying, skilful work is the father, Earth is the mother of all economic value. However this may be, money does not have value of its own; money doesn't create value; money mediates the exchange of economic values.

Given the informational nature of money, it is not surprising to find differences over what is defined as money. There is ongoing expert dispute over this, dating back at least to the 1840s' controversy between the currency school and the banking school. Today, in the advanced conditions of the Information Age, the potential for confusion is all the greater.

For example, consider a traditional savings account, perhaps documented in an old-fashioned savings booklet. People's understanding of savings quite often represents it as a sort of piggy bank. We think we have put money into the savings account, and there it is, being stored until we take it out. We would probably say, "I have some money in this account". In reality, things are different.

A first approximation could be to say we have lent the bank our savings. The money is not in the account, but the bank is working with it. The bank may in turn have lent our money to someone else, so that the money keeps circulating, while the credit note in the savings booklet confirms our claim to be paid back that money. Thus, such a savings deposit is clearly an asset, but it is not money instantly available for transactional purposes. One cannot usually pay with a savings booklet.

This first approximation, realistic as it may seem to be, is not really correct. Nowadays, most people don't usually deposit cash directly into a savings account. We usually transform a sight deposit into a savings deposit, by transferring it from our current account into our savings account. By doing so, seen from the bank's point of view, we convert a very short-term liability of the bank into a somewhat longer-term liability. In other words, we convert sight deposits, which the bank is obliged to pay out any time on demand, into savings deposits, which are only partly payable on demand – the rest not being available until after a several weeks' or months' period of notice.

The amount of money available to a bank does not change through any such operation. This is counterintuitive but true. For the most part, under today's arrangements, banks don't need as much money as might be supposed. Contrary to what most people think, a bank does not "work with the money" on customers' accounts, any more than it works with the notes in people's wallets. A bank works with the cash in its own till and, more importantly, with relatively small amounts of money in its own account with the central bank. Very often banks can settle supposed

Table 1
SYNOPSIS OF MONETARY TERMS, SIMPLIFIED

	Gold[1]	Coins	Notes	Sight deposits = Non-cash money	Time deposits	Savings deposits	Further such depos.	Securities, Bonds, Equity, or others
Monetary "Container"	Nostalgic display cabinet	Pocket, purse or wallet		Current account	Special accounts[2] = Short-term capital accounts			Capital accounts
Monetary aggregate		M0						
				M1				
						M2		
							M3 / M4	
Monetary status	Out of circulation	Circulating Money = Instant full liquidity = Means of payment for transaction purposes = medium of exchange			"Near-money" = Not money = Short-term capital = "store of value"			Long-term capital = "store of value"

1) or any other material commodity such as land, industrial plants, goods, resources/energy.

2) Accounts with limited or no access. Deposits not available until agreed maturity up to 2 years (time deposits) or redeemable at notice up to three months (traditional savings accounts). Increasingly, however, such accounts offer availability of money any time. Nevertheless such deposits have to be converted into a sight deposit before cashless payments can be carried out.

transfers of money by pure clearance of claims and liabilities among customers' accounts.

For example, when person A pays £100 to person B, the bank deducts 100 units representing £100 from the current account of A, and adds the same figure to the current account of B. Person A has paid his or her debt, person B has received the payment, but the bank has not moved a single penny. Only when a customer wants to be paid in cash, then the bank has to pay out money from its till; or when transfers have to be carried out to banks in distant locations or abroad (which is differently organised in different countries), then the bank has to transfer, i.e. actually pay out non-cash money from its account with the central bank. But even in such a case a bank's money reserves can be relatively small, because money that has to be paid out to customers at other banks is counterbalanced by money paid in to its own customers.

The banking system is two-tiered. Current accounts of customers are maintained at and managed by a bank, whereas current accounts of banks are maintained and managed at the central bank. Deposits of the banks with the central bank are not actually called sight deposits on current accounts, though that is what they are, but bankers' deposits on operational accounts, also referred to as operational reserves (called excess reserves outside the UK). These reserves are created by the central bank. They are official central bank money – the official currency of a central bank – like the legal tender it has issued as banknotes.

Banks can also have current accounts with other banks, as customers and partners of each other. The term sight deposit usually only refers to current accounts that customers maintain with a bank (also called demand deposit, checking deposit, or overnight deposit). Sight deposits are created by commercial banks. In that sense, they are a kind of private money, a parallel means of payment which is not strictly "currency" like banknotes and coins, but is denominated in official currency and used as if it were currency.

How then do central banks create operational reserves, and how do banks create sight deposits? Both do it in the same way, by lending money to their customers. They simply write a double entry into the bank's accounts – one as a credit entry on the asset side, the other one as a debit entry on the liability side. The bank's credit entry is matched by the customer's liability to pay interest on the loan and repay it later, while the bank's debit entry is matched by a credit entry in the customer's account. The same mechanism is actuated whenever a customer makes use of his or her overdraft facility. The customer gets the money and a debt, whereas the bank has a claim to be paid interest on the debt and be repaid it later, together with a liability to pay the customer the sum of money involved in the overdraft.

Table 2
MONETARY AGGREGATES

Cash	=	coin + banknotes
M0	=	cash + bankers' operational deposits
M1	=	cash + customers' sight deposits
M2	=	M1 + time deposits (up to two years) + savings deposits
M3	=	M2 + money market fund shares/units + debt securities (up to 2 years)
M4	=	cash + all types of retail and wholesale deposits including building society deposits
M	=	cash in public circulation + banks' cash + sight deposits (i.e. all chequeable deposits) + a fraction of bankers' operational deposits.

Various laws and other precautionary rules are designed to limit an otherwise unlimited free creation of money by the banks. These rules aim to formulate ceilings of new credit, e.g. in relation to capital reserves, or ratios between short-term and long-term liabilities. There are many such rules, quite complicated. But in the end they do not really limit credit creation because it is relatively easy for the banking sector as a whole to build up the assets it needs in order to match the liabilities it wants. Almost any outflow from the banking sector is, after all, an inflow to some other part of the banking sector.

This analysis enables us to see, in spite of the complexities, that the stock of money in circulation consists of a cash component and a non-cash component. The cash component is all the coins and banknotes; the non-cash component is customers' sight deposits and banks' operational deposits. Table 1 (see opposite page) contains a synopsis of such categories.

There are two questions here which are controversial. First, do gold and silver belong to the cash? Second, do banks' operational deposits belong to the same category as customers' sight deposits and add to the stock of money?

In legal principle, pure gold and silver continue in most countries to be valid money. If an authorized issuing institution has stamped its seal upon them, they are even recognized as legal tender. So they may for a while still be considered as an asset, a valuable "reserve", however volatile its value tends to be. In practice and as a matter of fact, gold and silver are no longer used as a means of payment. Accordingly, they are no longer part of the stock of money in circulation.

As regards non-cash, the two-tier banking system comes with a twofold circulation of money: one being the public circulation of sight deposits; the other being the interbank circulation of operational reserves. In terms of set-theory, banks' operational deposits represent a sub-set of customers' and banks' sight deposits. There is some interaction between the two circuits when it comes to settling final payments between banks in money held by the central bank, after all possible clearances (i.e. cancellings out) of sight deposits have been completed within banks and between banks. Nevertheless there is no exchange of units between the two circuits. They don't mingle with one another at all.

The circulation pattern of cash is different. Coin and notes circulate everywhere, and cash can move from one of these cicuits to the other. But it does not play a basic role any more. The time when operational and sight deposits were derivatives of cash ended when the gold standard and the last remnants of gold core currencies were abandoned. That happened between 1931 (in Britain) and 1971 (in the USA). Since then, the relationship between cash and non-cash has been reversed. Basically, now, money is purely informational; it is the kind of non-cash money that takes the form of bankers' operational deposits and customers' sight deposits on current accounts. Cash can be withdrawn from these deposits and they may be downloaded on to a cash-card; and cash may be paid into these accounts. But it has now become a secondary, subordinate form of money, with non-cash as the primary, more important form.

The fact that interbank and public circulation do not mingle means that, under the fractional reserve system, operational reserves are not included in the stock of circulating money. The same applies to the cash in the banks' tills, and also to foreign exchange. If cash or foreign exchange are deposited by a customer, the customer gets a sight deposit in exchange, and that is included in the stock of money. If a bank's cash comes directly from the central bank, the cash is delivered as a loan granted to the bank by the central bank. So the cash represents central bank money in the interbank circulation.

The official measure of the stock of money in public circulation is captured in the monetary aggregate called M1 (M-1B in America). M1 is made up of cash in public circulation plus sight deposits. It does not include operational deposits, nor the cash in the banks' tills, and for the same reason foreign exchange is excluded too. The recent amount of M1 in different countries and its annual growth can be seen in the first five columns of Table 3 at the end of this Appendix.

"Reserves" in the fractional reserve system are measured in the monetary aggregate M0. It consists of the total of central bank money, called base money, including notes and coin plus non-cash currency in the form of bankers' operational reserves (Table 2).

Further types of deposits include savings deposits and time deposits (with an agreed notice period), or items on other accounts such as securities, bonds and equity shares. All of these represent financial capital, not money, because they are not regularly used as a means of payment. The only type of deposit that serves transactional purposes, i.e. with which one is able to make regular cashless payments, are sight deposits. All other types of deposits are not directly chequeable. They serve investment purposes primarily aimed at earning interest. Thus they represent capital deposits on capital accounts (Table 1).

That is why the monetary aggregate M2 (as in the USA and the Euro area, formerly also in Britain) is not a measure of the stock of circulating money, but an aggregate statistical indicator lumping together the stock of money in public circulation (M1) with different stocks of interest-bearing short-term capital such as savings and time deposits, and in the USA money market paper too. The same applies to M3 in the USA and the Euro area as well as to M4 in Britain. They include other types of deposits and securities in addition to M2 (Table 2).

Definitions of monetary aggregates have varied according to time and country. The reason for the apparent arbitrariness concerning the definition of money and capital lies in the predominance of the microperspective of bankers' accountancy. In such a perspective, sight deposits, time deposits, savings deposits, etc, could seem to be just various types of short-term liabilities. Sight deposits on current accounts are not seen as fundamentally different from the rest, in that only they are chequeable for cashless payments.

Seen from a banking view, short-term capital appears to be "near-money", with the boundaries between capital and sight deposits and cash becoming increasingly blurred. For example, in most countries withdrawals of limited amounts from the savings deposits in M2 can be made on demand. NOW-accounts (Negotiable Orders of Withdrawal) offered by U.S. savings banks can be withdrawn completely at any time. More and more banks in America and Europe now offer special arrangements for interest-bearing time deposits, although formally deposits redeemable at notice, to be in fact redeemable on demand. The money is immediately available to the customer. But it is not part of the circulating stock of money included in M1 because the "near-money" itself is not used as a regular means of payment. Before a cashless payment can be made with it, it must be transformed into a sight deposit on a current account, from where it can be transferred as a payment. Once it is on the current account, it is included under M1.

So any savings or time deposit, even if it is completely and instantly available to the customer, remains short-term capital and does not formally add to M1. In practice, however, much of the "near-money" does now represent instant liquidity almost as if it were money. This is probably why M1 in the U.S. has not been growing as usual but even shrinking during certain years since the beginning of the 1990s (Table 3), whereas M2 and M3 have continued to grow faster. Sight deposits are apparently created only when needed for carrying out payments, and are extinguished immediately thereafter by the receiver transforming them into interest-bearing short-term capital. That being so, a considerable proportion of the short-term capital now recorded under M2 – on average at least 30%, probably more, of the entire amount of non-chequeable deposits under that heading – could reasonably be estimated as more appropriate to M1.

In short, if there was an absolutely clear dividing line between money and capital (which, in the existing reserve system there is not), the statistics would show that much of the short-term capital in today's M2, i.e. non-chequeable deposits with unlimited access, should be counted as money (M1) in addition to the existing stock of money in circulation.

A.2 Defining and Estimating the Money Stock After Seigniorage Reform

Let us call the total stock of existing official money M. Today, M can be understood as the stock of actually existing money which has been created either by the central bank or by private commercial banks. Even if a certain portion of this money is not in public circulation, it is nevertheless operationally necessary and needs to be created. After seigniorage reform, when the central bank will have the exclusive prerogative of creating the entire stock of official money, M will represent more clearly the quantity of plain money in existence. It will provide the base-line for deciding the amount of new money to be created annually, and therefore the amount of seigniorage revenue it will generate.

To estimate future M after seigniorage reform, we start from today's M. It can be measured as the whole set of M0 and M1. This includes all existing cash, not excluding the cash in the banks'. tills. It also includes that part of the operational reserves in M0 which serve the banks' own business; the other part which serves to carry out customer payments belongs to the sight deposits under M1. For simplicity we estimate that 50% of the bankers' operational deposits serve the banks' own business, and that the rest serves as a payment reserve for customers' transfers of sight deposits to banks at other locations and abroad. Today, these operational reserves are of functional rather than numerical importance. They fulfil an important function in the system but the amounts are small (see Table 3, column D).

Starting, then, from today's M as including M0 + M1 (i.e. cash in public circulation + all sight deposits + banks' cash + say, 50% of bankers' operational deposits), we need to add another two items to get an estimate of future M after seigniorage reform. One, as discussed above, is the conservatively estimated 30% of today's M2 deposits which can be transferred on demand to current accounts for use as payments. These 30% will be formally held as what, for practical purposes, they already are, i.e. non-cash money (Table 3, column E).

The other item to be added arises as follows. After seigniorage reform there will still be a two-tier banking system, but no twofold circulation of non-cash money. Existing clearance practices will no doubt be continued for practical reasons, but these will no longer merely substitute for paying money. They will have become payments in non-cash money among current accounts, no matter whether these are bank accounts or customer accounts and where they are located. As a result, banks will have to handle much more money on their operational accounts with their central bank in carrying out their loan-broking and investment business. This will probably make it necessary for them to hold more money on those accounts, certainly much more than the negligible sums of today. The total could correspond to 50% of today's cash in the banks' tills. That amount is shown in column F of Table 3.

At first glance, bankers could see it as a hardship to have suddenly to make sure they have significantly more money in stock. But it would be offset by the central bank probably releasing the banks' minimum reserves that have been obligatory under the present system. In 1998/99 obligatory minimum reserves amounted to £1.6 billion in the UK, €105 billion in the Eurozone, and $43.4 billion in the USA. With the fractional reserve system coming to an end, there would no longer be any justification to impose obligatory reserves for the safety of sight deposits. And safeguarding against bad loans is a different task for which there are different safety regulations already being in force. In countries where high minimum reserves are now held, the pay-back of obligatory reserves by the central bank to the banks might have to be stretched out. In countries with no minimum reserves today, e.g. Denmark or Sweden, or countries with very little reserve requirements, banks might be offered a transitional special-purpose low-interest loan facility instead. In this way it may be possible to sugar the pill for the banks in those countries. The banks in countries with normal or high minimum reserves will in principle face no problem.

Even if the estimates given here may become subject to revision, the approach above will remain valid. It suggests that the stock of future M and its annual growth will on average be greater than the stock and growth of today's M1.

A.3 Estimating Today's Special Banking Profits

Today's way of creating new non-cash money is doubly disadvantageous. It imposes unnecessary "money taxes" in the form of special banking profits from interest paid on the stock of money (Chapter 4.1, 4.7), and it fails to collect seigniorage revenue as public revenue (Chapter 2.1). So the advantages of seigniorage reform will be the benefit of no longer having to pay interest for special banking profits and the benefit of seigniorage revenue. The total benefit of seigniorage reform to the real economy will include both.

The special banking profit for both central bank and commercial banks does not consist of the amount of money created, because the banks do not create that money for their own use (which would be unlawful). The central bank creates operational reserves for the banks, not for itself; the banks create sight deposits as money for the customers, not for the issuing banks themselves. Credit created appears in the banks' balance sheet as an asset as well as a liability. Whenever a loan is paid back, the corresponding assets and deposits disappear on both sides of the balance sheet – as described in the reflux-principle by the representative of the 19th century banking school, John Fullarton. The credit created would certainly represent a decent seigniorage, but banks don't have seigniorage. Instead, they have a special profit from interest paid on the credit they create. The special profit may be greater or smaller than seigniorage would have been. X per cent interest for Y years on an amount of money M can add up to a lower or higher sum than M itself.

The yearly profit of central banks reflects the interest they receive from banks at home and abroad in respect of those banks' liabilities to the central bank. The profit is the surplus remaining after the expenses of a central bank have been subtracted. Such expenses are operating costs for salaries, services, transactions, etc., and interest payable by central banks to banks for temporarily re-borrowing (= absorbing) money from them. Table 4, line A, gives an international comparison of central banks' annual surplus. Depending on national differences, all or some part of the profit is delivered to the national treasury, with other parts flowing into different types of reserve funds. The Bank of England continues to be taxed on gross profit as if it still were a private sector commercial bank.

In contrast to central banks' surpluses, the commercial banks' special profits from creating sight deposits are not disclosed. Banks may not themselves know what they are. Their books are not designed to show such things. So how can we estimate what those special, supernormal profits are?

The special profits of commercial banks can be estimated by taking into account the composition of deposits and specific interest rates. We can assume that the debit-interest rates – the rates of interest which banks don't have to pay when they create new credit as loans to their customers, and which constitute their special profits – are roughly equal to the national base rate (e.g. repo rate, discount rate, etc). The structure of this approach is explained in more detail in table 4, footnote 3.

Depending on national particularities and the current stage of the interest rates cycle, the special banking profits of commercial banks seem to be about twice the size of central bank profits. If the use of cash decreases in the long term as foreseen, that will cause the banks' special profits to become accordingly higher. That tendency is counterbalanced to a certain degree in countries with large reserves of foreign exchange. By lending these, central banks earn capital market interest rates which are much higher than domestic base rates. The situation in the UK is different from other countries because the Bank of England shares holding of international reserves and foreign currency liquidity with the UK government. Elsewhere, foreign exchange is exclusively held by central banks.

Table 4, line C, shows the total of "money taxes", i.e. central banks' and commercial banks' special profits from the creation of operational and sight deposits. In 1998 these were $55.7bn in the USA, £23.9bn in the UK, DM45.3bn in Germany, and ¥4,087bn in Japan.

A.4 Estimating Seigniorage

With regard to future seigniorage, or today's seigniorage foregone, it needs to be understood that it is not identical with the annual addition to the stock of money M. Government revenue would not be increased by the entire amount of new money created. Three factors have to be taken into account: first, the amount of existing seigniorage from coining; second, a possible surplus in foreign exchange inflows; third, that part of central banks' annual net profit which comes from lending domestic currency (as contrasted with that part which comes from lending national stocks of foreign reserves).

The first item, seigniorage from coining, is already part of public revenue. Coining would continue to be part of the prerogative of creating official money, be it the government's or the central bank's. That part of seigniorage would continue to exist, but since it is not foregone today it would not be additional revenue after seigniorage reform. The amount is of minor importance. Coin represents about 1.5% of M1, and less in an increasingly cashless future.

The second factor, a possible surplus of foreign exchange inflows, certainly accounts for more. In countries with a surplus in the foreign exchange balance, potential seigniorage revenue would be reduced according to the annual increase of foreign exchange reserves. The reason is that in a national territory only national currency is admitted. An income from abroad has to be converted at home into national currency. In the case of the transnational European Monetary Union the principle is the same. The conversion is carried out by the central bank which takes in the foreign exchange as an asset in exchange for currency of the realm. This means creation of additional domestic currency to the extent to which external payments in and out result in a surplus in the foreign exchange balance. A positive net balance results in an addition to M1 and M. Those who receive the new domestic money are not the government, but the institutions and private persons who have taken in the foreign exchange.

In countries with a foreign exchange surplus, the amount of seigniorage that will be lost is not negligible, but not too significant either. For example, in the UK in the middle of the 1990s the balance of external financial flows was on average £2.7bn, varying between -9.4 in 1994 and +13.1 in 1997. On average this represents 7% of the average annual growth of M1, which was around £40bn (Colquhoun 1999: 365). In Germany at the same time the situation was similar. Growth of M1 on a three-year average was about DM60bn, whereas the increase of foreign exchange reserves was on average DM 4.2 billion, representing about 7% of M1 (Bundesbank Monatsberichte, tables II.2, III.1).

A foreign exchange deficit, conversely, does not reduce seigniorage. To be more precise, it does not do so for the moment. But it will do later when the deficit is closed by a temporary foreign exchange surplus. Then the central bank will create more of the new money by converting foreign exchange and less by creating seigniorage than it otherwise would. Under conditions of overall international growth with growing stocks of money everywhere the problem is not very relevant. If, however, a national deficit is chronic and growing, this has serious consequences for the national economy. Most foreign business partners will not accept payment in a currency in chronic deficit, usually under the strain of domestic inflation and international depreciation. They prefer to settle business in one of the hard currencies. That is why excessive "printing" of new money can never be a sustainable option. It leads inevitably almost without delay to domestic inflation and lethal implosion of a currency's external value.

Thirdly, as a consequence of seigniorage reform, governments will lose part of the revenue they now get from their share of the central banks' special banking profits from creating debt-money. The domestic part of these profits will no longer exist after seigniorage reform. So it must be deducted when we calculate the addition to public revenue that seigniorage reform will yield. This does not apply to the entire central bank's profit, just that part of it which stems from interest on loans it has made in its own national currency.

Since a fundamental restructuring of the world monetary system, including the question of repatriation of foreign excess reserves, cannot be expected to happen in a foreseeable future, central banks will continue to make profits from lending the accumulated national stocks of foreign exchange reserves, and those profits will continue to contribute to the public purse. For simplicity we estimate the domestic and the foreign part of central banks' profit each to be roughly 50% of the total

If we want to know now in numbers how much money seigniorage and public revenue will be, we start from the fact that today's governments already have some revenue from the creation of money. The annual amount of it is the sum of new coin plus the total of central bank's net profit delivered to the public purse (Table 4, line F).

The annual value of seigniorage will come from issuing the annual addition to M. As we have said, it is not to be confused with the special profits of today's commercial banks that arise from interest income on additions to M1. So annual seigniorage revenue foregone today can be calculated by starting from the annual addition to M and then subtracting interest on lending the foreign exchange surplus as well as the value of new coin (Table 4, line G). The total of public revenue foregone, however, is less than seigniorage foregone because of the profits governments now receive from their central bank (Table 4, line H).

Future seigniorage will include almost all of future additions to M as calculated in Table 3, except for any surplus of foreign exchange which will have to be deducted from them (Table 4, line I). Then, to get the total of future public revenue from the creation of money, it will be necessary to add whatever profit there may be from lending foreign reserves (Table 4, line J).

All the figures given in Tables 3 and 4, except the actual amount of M1, should be regarded as approximate calculations. Their purpose is to obtain an idea of the amounts of money seigniorage reform is about. A more detailed and statistically more precise calculation would no doubt yield revised figures, but they could be expected to be of a similar order. Annual amounts of seigniorage revenue depend, for the most part, on the scale of the annual additions to M1, and these have differed widely from one year to another.

The message of these calculations is unequivocal. Seigniorage reform will bring a substantial pay-off. The total additional annual revenue governments can expect to get from seigniorage and remaining central bank profits would, given existing price structures, be of the order of £49bn in the UK, $114bn in the USA, more than €160 in the Euro area, and ¥17.4 trillion in Japan. People in general will benefit more than that. They will be able to build up higher savings and capital of their own, because they will enjoy lower tax burdens or improved public services and the relief of no longer paying interest on the stock of domestically created official money. Seigniorage reform will be good for almost everybody.

Table 3

The Stock of Money in Circulation. Recent growth of M1, today's M, and M after seigniorage reform in the USA, UK, Euro area, Germany, and Japan. [Billion units. Non-statistical explanations see accompanying text]

| | M1 Today | | | | | M under present conditions | | | | | Future M after seigniorage reform | | | | | |
	A Cash[1]	B Sight deposits[2]	A+B =M1	ΔM1	ΔM1 3 years average	C Banks' cash[3]	D Oper. Deposits 50%	C+D +M1 = M	ΔM	ΔM 3 years average	E 30% of M2-spec deposits[4]	F Future oper. deposits[5]	E+F +M = Future M	Future ΔM[6]	Future ΔM 3 years average	
USA US Dollar																
1990	247	578	825			186	0.83	1,012			736	93	1,841			1990
1991	267	630	897	72		186	0.51	1,084	72		745	93	1,922	81		1991
1992	293	732	1,025	128		186	0.58	1,212	128		723	93	2,028	106		1992
1993	322	807	1,129	104	101	193	0.53	1,323	111	104	708	97	2,128	100	96	1993
1994	354	796	1,150	21	84	182	0.58	1,333	10	83	706	91	2,130	2	69	1994
1995	372	755	1,127	-23	34	194	0.65	1,310	-23	33	757	97	2,164	34	45	1995
1996	394	688	1,082	-45	-16	201	0.71	1,284	-26	-13	823	101	2,208	44	27	1996
1997	424	651	1,075	-7	-25	228	0.84	1,304	20	-10	892	114	2,310	102	60	1997
1998	459	635	1,094	19	-11	217	0.79	1,312	8	1	992	109	2,413	103	83	1998
1999	505	604	1,109	15	9	236	0.66	1,346	34	21	1,056	118	2,520	107	104	1999

1 4–6 % of which are coin, 94 - 96% banknotes.
2 Sight deposits = overnight deposits = all chequeable deposits
3 If source data are not available, banks's cash is accounted at 15% of currency.
4 M2-specific deposits = M2 – M1. M2 in USA = M1 + Retail MMMFs + Savings + Small Time Deposits. In Europe without MMMFs (Money Market Fund shares/fund units/paper).
5 50% of today's cash in the banks' till
6 Future ΔM = the potential of seigniorage if it existed today.

Table 3: Continued

	M1 Today					M under present conditions					Future M after seigniorage reform					
	A Cash[7]	B Sight deposits[8]	A+B =M1	ΔM1	ΔM1 3 years average	C Banks' cash[9]	D Oper. Deposits 50%	C+D +M1 = M	ΔM	ΔM 3 years average	E 30% of M2-spec deposits[10]	F Future oper.[11]	E+F +M = Future M	Future ΔM[12]	Future ΔM 3 years average	
UK Sterling																
1993[13]	20.4	194	214			3.1		217			54	1.5	273	.		1993
1994	21.7	200	222	8		3.3		225	8		56	1.6	283	10		1994
1995	23.2	224	247	25		3.5		251	26		57	1.7	310	27		1995
1996	24.7	241	266	19	17	3.7		270	19	17	59	1.8	331	21	19	1996
1997	26.3	313	339	73	39	4.0	0.08	343	73	39	96	2.0	441	110	53	1997
1998	27.8	339	367	28	40	4.2	0.13	371	28	40	105	2.1	478	37	56	1998
1999[14]	29.3	389	418	51	51	4.4	0.09	422	51	51	101	2.2	525	47	65	1999
Euro area																
1997[15]	311	1,284	1,595			52		1,647			618	26	2,291			1997
1998	324	1,453	1,777	182		59		1,836	189		635	30	2,501	210		1998
1999[16]	329	1,543	1,872	95		62	0.35	1,934	98		638	31	2,603	102		1999

7 4–6% of which are coin, 94–96% banknotes.

8 Sight deposits = overnight deposits = all chequeable deposits

9 If source data are not available, banks's cash is accounted at 15% of currency.

10 M2-specific deposits = M2 – M1. M2 in USA = M1 + Retail MMMFs + Savings + Small Time Deposits. In Europe without MMMFs (Money Market Fund shares/fund units/paper).

11 50% of today's cash in the banks' till

12 Future ΔM = the potential of seigniorage if it existed today.

13 1993-96 Notes and coin + non-interest-bearing + interest-bearing sight deposits (Mon.Finan.Stat., table 12.1). 1997-99 M1 of the EMS for the UK.

14 October 1999

15 March 1998 first available figure

16 October 1999

Table 3: Continued

	M1 Today					M under present conditions					Future M after seigniorage reform					
	A Cash[17]	B Sight deposits[18]	A+B =M1	ΔM1	ΔM1 3 years average	C Banks' cash[19]	D Oper. Deposits 50%	C+D +M1 = M	ΔM	ΔM 3 years average	E 30% of M2-spec deposits[20]	F Future oper. deposits[21]	E+F +M = Future M	Future ΔM[22]	Future ΔM 3 years average	
Germany Deutsche Mark																
1992	227	469	696	70	77	23.9	0.59	720			318	12	1,050			1992
1993	239	514	753	57	49	27.8	0.39	781	61		354	14	1,149	99		1993
1994	251	538	789	36	54	26.2	0.41	816	35		352	13	1,181	32		1994
1995	264	579	842	53	49	27.3	0.42	870	54	50	357	14	1,241	60	64	1995
1996	276	670	946	104	64	30.3	0.43	977	107	65	379	15	1,371	130	74	1996
1997	247	691	938	-8	50	30.8	0.37	969	-8	51	396	15	1,380	9	66	1997
1998	242	762	1,004	66	54	29.9	0.31	1,034	65	55	437	15	1,486	106	82	1998
1999²³	242	792	1,034	30	29	26.6	0.21	1,061	27	28	435	13	1,509	23	46	1999

17 4–6 % of which are coin, 94–96% banknotes.

18 Sight deposits = overnight deposits = all chequeable deposits

19 If source data are not available, banks's cash is accounted at 15% of currency.

20 M2-specific deposits = M2 – M1. M2 in USA = M1 + Retail MMMFs + Savings + Small Time Deposits. In Europe without MMMFs (Money Market Fund shares/fund units/paper).

21 50% of today's cash in the banks' till

22 Future ΔM = the potential of seigniorage if it existed today.

23 August 1999

Table 3: Continued

	M1 Today					M under present conditions					Future M after seignorage reform					
	A Cash[24]	B Sight deposits[25]	A+B =M1	ΔM1	ΔM1 3 years average	C Banks' cash[26]	D Oper. Deposits 50%	C+D +M1 = M	ΔM	ΔM 3 years average	E 30% of M2-spec deposits[27]	F Future oper. deposits[28]	E+F +M = Future M	Future ΔM[29]	Future ΔM 3 years average	
Japan Yen																
1990	34,443	85,518	119,961			5,166		125,127			95,753	2,583	223,463			1990
1991	35,263	94,371	129,634	9,673		5,289		134,923	9,796		95,643	2,645	233,211	9,748		1991
1992	36,040	96,064	132,104	2,470		5,406		137,510	2,587		94,466	2,703	234,679	1,468		1992
1993	37,505	99,132	136,637	4,533	5,559	5,626		142,263	4,753	5,703	95,063	2,813	240,139	5,460	5,559	1993
1994	39,074	104,281	143,355	6,718	4,574	5,861		149,216	6,953	4,764	97,137	2,931	249,284	9,145	5,358	1994
1995	41,646	120,043	161,689	18,334	9,862	6,247		167,936	18,720	10,142	96,776	3,124	267,836	18,552	11,051	1995
1996	44,789	133,078	177,867	16,178	13,743	6,718		184,585	16,649	14,107	96,706	3,359	284,650	16,814	14,837	1996
1997	48,905	144,759	193,664	15,797	16,770	7,336		201,000	16,415	17,261	98,091	3,668	302,759	18,109	17,825	1997
1998	50,937	153,792	204,729	11,065	14,347	7,641		212,370	11,370	14,811	101,046	3,821	317,237	14,478	16,467	1998

Sources: The Federal Reserve Board of the United States, **www.bog.frb.fed.us**, Releases, Historical data, tables 1, 2, Assets and liabilities of commercial banks in the United States/Cash assets; European Central Bank, **www.ecb.int**, Monthly Bulletins, tables 1.5, 2.4; Office for National Statistics, London, Monetary and Financial Statistics Division, **www.bankofengland.co.uk/mfsd**, tables 1, 3.2+3, 12.1, Base rate, 9.1; Deutsche Bundesbank, **www.bundesbank.de**, Monatsberichte, Tabelle II.2, IV.1, V.2; Bank of Japan, **www.boj.or.jp/en**, Long-term time-series data, Money stock (old basis), Central bank discount rates.

24 4–6 % of which are coin, 94–96% banknotes.

25 Sight deposits = overnight deposits = all chequeable deposits

26 If source data are not available, banks's cash is accounted at 15% of currency.

27 M2-specific deposits = M2 – M1.. M2 in USA = M1 + Retail MMMFs + Savings + Small Time Deposits. In Europe without MMMFs (Money Market Fund shares/fund units./paper).

28 50% of today's cash in the banks' till

29 Future ΔM = the potential of seigniorage if it existed today.

Table 4

SEIGNIORAGE AND SPECIAL BANKING PROFITS FROM THE CREATION OF MONEY [Billion units]

	USA $	Euro Area €	UK £	Germany DM	Japan ¥
A. Central bank annual surplus[1]	1997 20.8 1998 18.4	Data not yet available	1998[2] 2.50 1999[2] 2.74	1997 24.2 1998[2] 16.2	1999 2,241
B. Commercial banks' estimated special profit in 1998/99[3]	37.3	57.9	21.4	29.7	1,846
C. (A+B) Total of special banking profits in '98	55.7	—	23.9	45.3	4,087
D. Average annual ΔM[4] after seigniorage reform	105	156	42	65	16,294
E. (C+D) Possible relief of the real economy	160	—	66	110	20,381
Following figures as of '98 or '99					
F. Public revenue from money creation today[5]	18.7	—	2.92	17.2	2,407
G. Seigniorage foregone[6]	31.7	89.9	46.6	59.4	10,429
H. Public revenue foregone[7]	13.3	—	44.1	43.2	8188
I. Future seigniorage[8]	105	156	47	65	16,293
J. Future public revenue[9]	114	>160	48.5	75	17,414
K. Total of government tax revenue	2,331	2,932	298	1,074	81,809
L. (I : K) Current percentage of taxes replaceable by seigniorage	~ 4.5%	~ 5.3%	~ 15%	~ 6%	~ 19%

Sources: Federal Reserve Board of the United States, **www.bog.frb.fed.us**, Annual Report 1998. – European Central Bank, **www.ecb.int**, Annual Report 1998; Monthly bulletin, tables 5.1, 7.1. – Bank of England, **www.bankofengland.co.uk/mfsd**, Annual Report 1999. – Office for National Statistics, London, **www.ons.gov.uk**. – Deutsche Bundesbank, **www.bundesbank.de**, Geschäftsbericht 1998, Monatsberichte, table VIII.1. – Bank of Japan, **www.boj.or.jp/en**, Annual Report 1999, Bank of Japan Accounts; Central banks interest rates. – Japanese Tax Administration, **www.nta.go.jp**, Breakdown of General Account Revenue. – OECD in Figures 1999, **www.oecd.org/publications/figures**, pp.12, 38.

1 Interest receivable by central bank minus interest payable to banks, and minus operational expenses of central bank, necessary capital reserves, or similar.

2 Profits of the issue department payable to HM Treasury plus profits of the banking department.

3 Amounts are estimated as follows:
a) The special margin rate which earns the special banking profit from creation of sight deposits is in principle equal to the national base rate of x% (e.g. repo rate, discount rate, or similar). So the special profit on all non-interest bearing sight deposits SD in M1 = SD • x%.
b) A certain proportion of SD is interest-bearing to the customer. That interest of y% payable by the banks has to be subtracted from the base rate which is receivable by the banks.
c) Another proportion of SD is created by current overdrafts. On these, customers pay an additional extra interest rate of z% which has to be added to the base rate.
d) Composition of deposits and interest rates differ according to country. For simplicity's sake we assume that in all countries $3/4$ of chequeable deposits would be non-interest bearing, and $1/4$ interest-bearing (except in the UK, where the approx. proportion rather is $1/4$ to $3/4$), furthermore, $1/4$ of SD is currently created

by overdraft.
Interest rates could be accounted as follows: Base rate USA 5% – UK 5.5% – Euro area 3% – Japan 0.5%. Interest paid on sight deposits USA and UK 1.5%, Euro area 1%, Japan 0.3%. Additional overdraft rate USA and UK 5%, Euro area 4%, Japan 3%.
e) All in all, the special profits can be estimated at: $((2SD • x\%) + (SD • x+z\%) + (SD • x-y\%))/4$. In the UK: $((SD • x\%) + (SD • x-y+z\%) + (2SD • x-y\%)) / 4$.

4 Calculated for 1998 and 1999 as in table 3.

5 Coin (~1.5% of ΔM1) plus central bank net profit delivered to the public purse. Numbers in 5–9 as of 1998 or 1999.

6 ΔM minus foreign exchange surplus (~7% of ΔM1, except USA which has a deficit), minus new coin as above.

7 ΔM minus foreign exchange surplus as above, minus new coin as above, minus central bank net profit delivered to the public purse.

8 Future ΔM minus foreign exchange surplus as above.

9 Future ΔM minus foreign exchange surplus as above, plus interest from lending national stocks of foreign reserves (~50% of central bank net profit very roughly speaking).

LITERATURE

Armstrong, Alan 1996: *To Restrain The Red Horse*, Dunoon, Scotland: Towerhouse.

Bank of England 1996: *Introduction to Monetary Operations*, Centre for Central Banking Studies, Handbooks in Central Banking, No. 10.

Bank of England 1998a: *Banking Act Report, 1997/98*.

Bank of England 1998b: *Monetary Policy in the United Kingdom*, Fact Sheet, August 1998.

Bank of England 1999: Report of 29 April to the House of Commons Treasury Select Committee and the House of Lords Select Committee on the Monetary Policy Committeee of the Bank of England.

Birch, David 1999: "E-cash Issues: Electronic Cash is not just about Technology", Proceedings of the Hyperion Digital Money Forum '99, eds John Coleman and David Birch, *European Business Review* Vol 99, No 4, 1999, Bradford: MCB University Press.

Boyle, David 1999: *Funny Money: In Search of Alternative Cash*, London: Harper Collins.

Colquhoun, Andrew 1999: "The external balance sheet of the United Kingdom. Recent developments", *Bank of England Quarterly Bulletin*, Nov 1999, 365 – 372.

Commission on Global Governance 1995: *Our Global Neighbourhood*, Oxford: Oxford University Press.

de Maré, Eric 1999: *Labour or Liberty*, published by the author at Dynevor House, New Street, Painswick, Glos. GL6 6UN.

Douthwaite, Richard 1999: *The Ecology of Money*, Schumacher Briefing No.4, Foxhole/Dartington: Green Books.

Fisher, Irving 1935: *100% Money*, Works Vol. 11, ed. and introduced by William J. Barber, London: Pickering & Chatto, 1997.

Friedman, Milton 1948: "A Monetary and Fiscal Framework for Economic Stability", *The American Economic Review*, 38 (1948) 245–264, reprinted in: Friedrich A. Lutz/Lloyd W. Mints (Eds) 1951: *Readings in Monetary Theory*, Homewood, Ill. (Richard D. Irwin), 369 – 393; reprinted again in: M Friedman (Ed) 1953, *Essays in Positive Economics*, The University of Chicago Press, 133 – 156.

Friedman, Milton 1959: *A Program for Monetary Stability*, New York: Fordham University Press.

Friedman, Milton 1969a: "The Optimum Quantity of Money", in *The Optimum Quantity of Money and other Essays*, New York: Aldine de Gruyter, 1969, 1 – 68.

Friedman, Milton 1969b: "The Monetary Theory and Policy of Henry Simons", in: *The Optimum Quantity of Money and other Essays*, New York: Aldine de Gruyter, 1969, 81–94.

Friedman, Milton 1991: *Monetarist Economics*, Oxford, UK/Cambridge, Mass.: Basil Blackwell.

Galbraith, John Kenneth 1975: *Money: Whence it came, where it went*, London/New York: Penguin.

Gesell, Silvio 1958: *The Natural Economic Order*, London: Peter Owen. Germ. 1919: *Die natürliche Wirtschaftsordnung durch Freiland und Freigeld*, Arnstadt: Verlag Roman Gesell.

Gibb Stuart, James 1995: *The Money Bomb*, Glasgow: Ossian Publishers.

Gocht, Rolf 1975: *Kritische Betrachtungen zur nationalen und internationalen Geldordnung*, Berlin: Duncker & Humblot.

Goodhart, C.A.E. 1989: *Money, Information and Uncertainty*, London: Macmillan.

Hart, Albert G. 1935: "The Chicago Plan of Banking Reform", *The Review of Economic Studies*, 2 (1935) 104 – 116, reprinted in: Friedrich A. Lutz/Lloyd W. Mints (Eds) 1951: *Readings in Monetary Theory*, Homewood, Ill.: Richard D. Irwin, 437–456.

Hayek, Friedrich A. von 1978: *Denationalisation of Money. An Analysis of the Theory and Practice of Concurrent Currencies* (2nd edition, The Argument Refined), London: Institute of Economic Affairs.

Hixson, William F. 1991: *A Matter of Interest: Re-examining Money, Debt and Real Economic Growth*, London/Westport Conn.: Praeger.

Hixson, William F. 1997: *It's Your Money*, COMER Publications, 3284 Yonge Street, Suite 500, Toronto, M4N 3M7, Canada.

Horsmann, George 1988: *Inflation in the Twentieth Century. Evidence from Europe and North America*, New York: St.Martin´s Press/ Harvester Wheatsheaf.

Huber, Joseph 1999: *Plain Money. A Proposal for Supplying the Nations with the necessary Means in a modern Monetary System*, Martin-Luther-University Halle a.d. Saale, Graureiher 99–3. Also at http://www.soziologie.uni-halle.de/index.html.

Hutchinson, Frances / Burkitt, Brian 1997: *The Political Economy of Social Credit and Guild Socialism*, London/New York: Routledge

Kennedy, Margrit (1995): *Interest and Inflation-Free Money: Creating an Exchange Medium that Works for Everybody and Protects the Earth*, Philadelphia: New Society.

Keynes, John Maynard, 1930: *A Treatise on Money*, London: Macmillan.

King, Mervyn 1999: *Challenges For Monetary Policy: New And Old, paper for a Symposium on New Challenges for Monetary Policy*, Federal Reserve Bank of Kansas City, Jackson Hole, Wyoming, 27 August 1999, London: Bank of England.

Knapp, Georg Friedrich 1905: *Staatliche Theorie des Geldes (Chartal theory of money)*, Leipzig: Duncker & Humblot.

Mairet, Philip 1934: *The Douglas Manual*, London: Stanley Nott.

Mayo, Ed *et al* 1998: *Small Is Bankable: Community Reinvestment in the UK*, London: New Economics Foundation.

Morrison, Ron F. 1999: "The Erosion of Seigniorage on the National Currency", *The Social Crediter*, Vol. 78, No. 4, July/August 1999, 42–43.

Munson, Gorham 1945: *Aladdin's Lamp. The Wealth of the American People*, New York: Creative Age Press.

Pahlke, Jürgen 1970: *Steuerbedarf und Geldpolitik in der wachsenden Wirtschaft. Geldschöpfung als Mittel der Staatsfinanzierung*, Berlin: Walter de Gruyter.

Robertson, James 1999: *Monetary Policy And Fiscal Policy: The Question of Credit Creation*, Vol II – Evidence, HL Paper 96, 367–373, London: House of Lords. (Also presented to the Treasury Select Committee, House of Commons.)

Rowbotham, Michael 1998: *The Grip of Death*, Jon Carpenter Publishing, Spendlove Centre, Charlbury, Oxon OX7 3PQ.

Simons, Henry C. 1948: "A Positive Programme for Laissez Faire. Some Proposals for a Liberal Economic Policy", and: "Rules versus Authorities in Monetary Policy". Both articles in: H.C. Simons, *Economic Policy for a Free Society*, The University of Chicago Press, 1948. First published as "Rules...", *The Journal of Political Economy*, 44 (1936) 1–30. Reprinted in: Lutz, Friedrich A. / Mints, Lloyd W. (Eds) 1951: *Readings in Monetary Theory*, Homewood, Ill.: Richard D. Irwin, 337–368.

Skidelsky, Robert 1992: John Maynard Keynes: Vol 2, *The Economist as Saviour*, 1920–1937, London: Macmillan.

The Social Crediter, 16 Forth Street, Edinburgh, EH1 3LH.